DATE DUE

| | | | |
|---|---|---|---|
| | | | |
| | | | |
| | | | |
| | | | |
| | | | |
| | | | |
| | | | |
| | | | |
| | | | |
| | | | |
| | | | |
| | | | |
| | | | |

IN
AMERICAN
HISTORY

# THE INDUSTRIAL REVOLUTION IN AMERICAN HISTORY

Anita Louise McCormick

**Enslow Publishers, Inc.**

40 Industrial Road          PO Box 38
Box 398               Aldershot
Berkeley Heights, NJ 07922   Hants GU12 6BP
USA                      UK

http://www.enslow.com

**Library of Congress Cataloging-in-Publication Data**

McCormick, Anita Louise.
    The industrial revolution in American history / Anita Louise
McCormick.
        p.  cm. — (In American history)
    Includes bibliographical references and index.
    Summary: Traces the history of the industrial revolution from its roots
in eighteenth-century England, through its beginnings in the United
States, to its decline in the twentieth–century.
    ISBN 0-89490-985-1
    1. Industrial revolution—United States—Juvenile literature.
2. Industrial revolution—England—Juvenile literature. 3. Industries—
United States—History—Juvenile literature. [1. Industrial revolution—
United States. 2. Industrial revolution—England. 3. Industries—History.]
I. Title. II. Series.
HC105.M233  1998
338.0973—dc21

                                                    97-23479
                                                        CIP
                                                        AC

Printed in the United States of America

10 9 8 7 6

**To Our Readers:** We have done our best to make sure all Internet Addresses in
this book were active and appropriate when we went to press. However, the
author and the publisher have no control over and assume no liability for the
material available on those Internet sites or on other Web sites they may link to.
Any comments or suggestions can be sent by e-mail to comments@enslow.com or
to the address on the back cover.

**Illustration Credits:** Enslow Publishers, Inc., p. 56; National Archives, pp. 19,
37, 42, 53, 59, 87, 89, 91, 92, 99, 104, 109; Reproduced from the *Dictionary of
American Portraits*, published by Dover Publications, Inc., in 1967, pp. 8, 25, 29,
65, 77, 80, 101; Courtesy of Anita Louise McCormick, pp. 72, 116.

**Cover Illustrations:** National Archives.

# ★ CONTENTS ★

# A CENTURY OF PROGRESS

May 10, 1876, was an exciting day in Philadelphia. It was the opening day of the Centennial Exhibition—the first world's fair ever to be held in the United States.

Thousands of people from all walks of life came to Philadelphia's Fairmont Park to take part in the celebration. Politicians, scientists, inventors, writers, shopkeepers, and housewives crowded in through the gates. Dignitaries from many nations were there. The exhibitors, especially a group of American inventors who had worked for years to perfect their ideas and bring them into the marketplace, were anxious to show their work to all who came.

The Centennial Exhibition was billed as the "greatest spectacle ever presented to the vision of the Western World."[1] Many people felt that this magnificent fair, held at the birthplace of their nation's independence, was the event of a lifetime. They did not want to miss it. During the exhibition's run from

May to October, nearly 8 million people—one out of five Americans—came to see what their nation had accomplished. Everyone who attended the Centennial Exhibition had a chance to view some thirty thousand exhibits. So many people wanted to present their ideas and products that over two hundred buildings had to be erected to hold the exhibits. In all, the fairgrounds covered 450 acres.[2]

Items from every American state, as well as fifty foreign nations, were on display. Even countries as far away as China and Egypt participated. There was fine silk from the Far East, hand-carved furniture from Europe, and fancy china and pottery. In short, the fair showcased the best the world had to offer in the fields of art, science, and commerce. But among the most popular attractions at the 1876 Centennial Exhibition were the exhibits of technological innovation—all products of the Industrial Revolution.

Machinery Hall, a building that covered nearly twenty acres of the fairground, held the bulk of these new inventions. Fairgoers passing through the large hall could hardly believe what they saw. They marveled at gas stoves, typewriters, mimeograph machines, and many other inventions for the home and office that had recently come out on the market.

New kinds of industrial and agricultural equipment were also on display. There were machines for making everything from factory equipment to consumer goods such as shoes, envelopes, wallpaper, and cloth.

Among all the unique and diverse inventions, one machine in particular caught everyone's eye. It was the largest steam engine ever built—a thirty-foot monster that held the attention of everyone in the hall.

George Corliss stood at the base of the huge twenty-five hundred horsepower engine he had created. At his side stood America's president, Ulysses S. Grant, and the emperor of Brazil, Dom Pedro.

"Are you both ready?" Corliss asked. Both national leaders nodded their heads. "Then your Majesty will turn that handle."

As Emperor Pedro moved the handle, a loud hiss of steam escaped from the engine.

"Now, Mr. President, yours," Corliss said.[3]

President Grant turned the second handle as Corliss requested, allowing another loud hiss of steam to escape. Then the engine's large metal beams slowly began to move and the gigantic machine went into full operation.

The crowd cheered wildly. Nearly everyone was surprised by the volume of this mighty engine's rumbling, hissing, and chugging. They had never seen such a powerful machine before.

But this monster of steel, brass, and copper did much more than make noise and attract attention. It

*George Corliss amazed spectators at the 1876 Centennial Exhibition with his invention—the largest, most powerful steam engine ever built.*

had the power to drive every steam-powered machine in the building. As soon as it was turned on, it provided the energy necessary to spin cotton, saw logs, pump water, make shoes, print newspapers, manufacture envelopes, and perform hundreds of other tasks. The fairgoers were astounded.

Although the majority of inventions at Machinery Hall were not nearly as large as George Corliss's engine, some proved, in time, to be even more impressive. Alexander Graham Bell, an inventor who was working to find new ways to communicate by using electricity, attended the Centennial Exhibition. He brought a working model of his recently patented telephone to display.

When Emperor Dom Pedro saw the invention, he immediately wanted to try it. He picked up the telephone and held it to his ear. The emperor was so startled when he heard a voice come through the speaker that he dropped the telephone and exclaimed, "My God, it talks!"[4]

Thomas Alva Edison, another outstanding inventor of the late 1800s, also attended the Centennial Exhibition. Just twenty-nine years old at the time, Edison had recently begun building his now-famous laboratory in Menlo Park, New Jersey. His innovative work with electronics, which would help extend and improve communications throughout the world, was just starting to receive the recognition it deserved.

Edison brought two new telegraph machines that he had recently invented to the 1876 world's fair. The first of these was a quadruplex telegraph. It allowed four telegraph messages to be transmitted over a single line at the same time. The other was an automatic telegraph machine. It could read and interpret letters and numbers that had been punched into a long strip of paper tape, then transmit the desired message over a wire. The automatic telegraph could send messages six times faster than the best human telegraph operators of the time.

The magnificent displays at the Centennial Exhibition clearly demonstrated the progress that America had made in its first hundred years of independence. While the fair was billed as a celebration of America's accomplishments of the past century, it was much more than that. It proved to the world that the United States had finally arrived as a major industrial power that was ready to meet the challenges of the future.

## First Hundred Years of Industrialization

In its first hundred years of independence, the United States had gone through many changes. Its population had increased over ten times from around 4 million in 1790 to nearly 40 million in 1870. It was no longer the agricultural society it had been when the Declaration of Independence was signed in 1776. While farming was still a vital part of the American economy, the United States was quickly becoming an industrial nation. It was a nation that could not only mass-produce the products its people needed, but also produce enough surplus to export to other nations as well.

Not even the most farsighted inventors and businessmen of the late 1700s could have foreseen the dramatic changes that the Industrial Revolution would eventually bring. By 1900, it would transform the United States from an agricultural nation into one of the wealthiest industrial nations in the world.

America's industrialization was aided by the nation's abundant supply of natural resources. There was plenty of coal and water to power the factory machines. Iron ore for making iron and steel products could be mined in many areas. A limitless supply of lumber was available for building. And there was more than enough available farmland to feed the nation's growing population.

By the 1876 Centennial Exhibition, the United States was becoming a widely industrialized nation. Many different types of products were being produced by American factories. Most of America's industries were still located in the North, but even the Southern states that had been torn by the Civil War were slowly becoming more industrialized. They not only grew cotton, but, with the help of the Northern states, began to build Southern mills that would spin cotton into thread and weave it into cloth as well.

But the Industrial Revolution did not happen all at once. It progressed slowly, one step at a time. This progress was based on the ideas, inventions, innovations, and labor of thousands of people, many building on the work of those who went before them.

# THE REVOLUTION BEGINS

Before the Industrial Revolution, life was very different from how it is today. The majority of people lived on farms and raised their own food. Crops had to be planted, tended, and harvested by hand or with the help of farm animals. Very little farm machinery was available, and all of it was primitive by today's standards. It took the labor of everyone in the household—men, women, and children—to raise enough food for the family.

In the evenings, women and girls spun thread and wove it into cloth. They then used this material to make clothes, bedding, and other necessities. Men and boys crafted tools, utensils, and other items from metal and wood. If people needed something they could not provide for themselves, they got it from someone else in the community.

## The Industrial Revolution Began in Europe

During the 1700s, the population in Europe started to soar. To satisfy the increasing demand for food, agricultural experts worked to develop better farming methods that would make it possible for farmers to grow more food than ever before. Inventors designed new farm machines that sped up the process of planting and harvesting. These improvements later came to be known as the agricultural revolution.

Once these machines came into use, fewer people were needed to do farmwork. As a result, many farmers started to branch out into other occupations, such as spinning thread, weaving cloth, and blacksmithing. They sold or traded their products for food and other items they needed.

This move away from nearly everyone growing their own food and providing for their own needs and toward people specializing in trades and crafts was one of the first big steps on the road to industrialization.

## Industrialization of the Textile Industry

Cloth manufacturing was the first industry to be affected by the Industrial Revolution. Before the mid-1700s, all thread was spun by hand and all cloth was woven on home looms. Cloth merchants brought wool, cotton, or flax fibers to a home spinner, who spun them into thread on a spinning wheel or hand spinner. The merchant later returned to pay the spinner for his or her work, then took the thread to the home of a weaver. The weaver would weave the thread into cloth on a loom. The process of cloth making was very slow and depended entirely on human labor.

As the growing European population needed more cloth and as large orders for textiles continued to come in from overseas colonies, the demand for thread and finished cloth soon exceeded the ability of English spinners and weavers to manufacture it. So inventors tried to come up with a machine that could speed up the process.

The first of these machines, the flying shuttle, was invented in 1733 by British mechanic John Kay. A shuttle is a needlelike device that weavers use to move the thread across the piece of cloth. With a flying shuttle, home weavers could send the shuttle flying across the loom by merely pulling on a cord. This made it possible for them to weave much more cloth than they ever could before.

In the late 1760s, James Hargreaves invented the spinning jenny, a machine that was able to spin eight threads at one time. Around the same time, Richard Arkwright patented a new type of spinning machine known as the spinning frame. Arkwright's first spinning frames were powered by horses that were trained to walk on treadmills. Some of Arkwright's later models were powered by a water-driven wheel.[1]

But the spinning frame had one disadvantage. It was too large and heavy for spinners to use in their homes. So Arkwright had to build factories where workers could go to operate the new machines. The first of these spinning factories was built in Nottingham, England. Arkwright's factory buildings were much larger than what people of the time were used to seeing. One observer described Arkwright's factory in Derbyshire, England, as "a palace of enormous size, having at least a score of windows in a row and at least five or six stories in height."[2]

Before the start of the Industrial Revolution, it took approximately twelve spinners to make enough thread to keep one weaver busy. But spinning machines made more thread available than home weavers could possibly make into cloth. This situation posed a new challenge for inventors.

In 1785, Edmund Cartwright designed and built the first working model of a water-powered loom that could weave thread into cloth much faster than any home weaver could. As with the spinning frames, however, the looms were far too large to fit into private homes. Before long, people who wanted to earn their living by weaving had no choice but to go to work in a factory, which took away some of the independence they had enjoyed while working in their homes.

The lure of making a profit with the new machinery inspired many wealthy businessmen to invest in textile factories. Soon, textile factories could be seen along the banks of rivers and streams all over England. At the beginning of the Industrial Revolution, factories were powered by rivers. The pressure of the water, moving downstream turned large waterwheels and, thereby, furnished the power the machinery needed to operate.

## The Steam Engine Is Invented

The limitations of water power caused some inventors to look for a better alternative—an inexpensive, reliable source of power that would make it possible to build factories almost anywhere. Machinery powered by steam, some inventors felt, was the answer. The first commercially successful steam engine was invented by Thomas Newcomen in 1712. It was later improved by James Watt, who found a way to get more work out of the engine while using the same amount of power. Newcomen's engines were powered by coal, which was used to heat water to the point where it produced powerful steam. Science writer Isaac Asimov said,

> The steam engine, bringing the use of energy to all mechanical devices in far greater quantity than anything else had offered in the past was the key to all that followed . . . when the face of the world was changed as drastically (and far more rapidly) than at any time since the invention of agriculture, nearly ten thousand years before.[3]

In the late 1780s, only a few factories were experimenting with steam power. As the word got around that steam engines worked, steam-powered factories, which could be built almost anywhere, started showing up all over England.

## The Change in People's Lives

The Industrial Revolution drastically changed the way many people lived and worked. Till then, most people worked together as families on the farm. Some people worked from home in cottage industries, where they added to their income by making products, weaving, or spinning. As soon as children were old enough to help, they worked alongside their parents. In those times, only the children of well-to-do families were sent to school. Education was a luxury that few people could afford.

Unemployed spinners, weavers, and farmers were among the first to work in English factories. These people were used to working long hours every day. But unlike when they were working for themselves, they were not able to schedule their own hours and take a break whenever they wanted. Supervisors required them to perform their tasks on a rigid schedule. Factory bosses told them when they could eat, drink, and rest. Few breaks were allowed. Working

*As huge numbers of people moved from the farms to the cities in order to be closer to their workplaces, finding good housing quickly became a problem. This photograph shows a family in front of a dilapidated home in Kansas City.*

conditions were usually much worse than they were at home or on the farm.

For all those reasons, many people found factory work very tiring and monotonous. But in the new industrial age, it was the only way that many people could make a living.

As the Industrial Revolution spread throughout England, much of the nation's population moved into factory towns to be closer to their place of employment. With this influx of people, housing shortages soon became a problem. A few factory owners tried to keep the living conditions of their workers as pleasant as possible by building housing units near their factories. But many did not. They paid their employees as little as possible, forcing them to live in poorly constructed houses with rats, insects, and other unsanitary conditions.

In the late 1700s, the people of England were still trying to adjust to the changes that industrialization was bringing to their nation. But even as they tried to fit into the new system, the benefits and drawbacks of this new way of doing things had already spread beyond their borders. Several other European nations, including Germany and France, were starting to become industrialized—and so was the United States of America.

In the late 1700s, a group of businessmen from New England became interested in building textile factories in the United States. They sent several representatives to England to try and recruit people who had the skills to build such plants. It had

# INDUSTRY IN AMERICA

not been long since the United States won its freedom from England in the Revolutionary War. When England's government and business leaders heard about the plan, they were not pleased. They did not want American textile mills to compete with them for business.

In order to keep America and other nations out of the textile business, the British government passed a law forbidding any spinning or weaving machinery, as well as anyone who had knowledge of such machines, to leave the country. But despite their best efforts, the English could not keep the inventions that made the mass production of textiles possible away from the rest of the world forever.

Samuel Slater, a mill supervisor in Lancaster, England, was the first textile expert to reach America's shores. Slater had been involved in the textile industry since he was fourteen years old. At that time, he had signed papers that made him an apprentice to Jedediah Strutt. This arrangement lasted for six and a half years. During that time, he worked for Strutt and was trained in his craft. After that, he was free to do what he wanted.

The working conditions at the mill where Slater worked were better than most in England. Jedediah Strutt had known Slater's father before he died. Strutt treated Slater like a son and took him into his home in Milford.

While working for Jedediah Strutt, Slater studied how the textile machines were made. He saw ways to improve them. As his apprenticeship neared its end, Slater started to think about his future. He wondered if his life would improve if he went to America.

Slater knew that his knowledge of textile machinery would be much more valuable in America than it was in England. Slater had heard that there were many businessmen in America who wanted to start textile mills. They were willing to pay good money to anyone who could help them. But due to British law, the machinery and knowledge the

Americans needed remained on the other side of the Atlantic Ocean.

So Slater thought about how he could make the trip. If he were to come to America, he would have to avoid being detected by British authorities. Still, he felt it was a risk worth taking.

When Slater was twenty-one, his apprenticeship ended. Having fulfilled his commitment to Strutt, Slater put his plan to go to America into action. It was too risky to take any written or drawn plans on the voyage, so he set out to memorize how spinning and weaving machines were put together.

In September 1789, Slater disguised himself as a farmer and boarded a ship bound for the United States. He arrived in America with little money, but with the knowledge that would revolutionize the way textiles were made.

Within a few weeks of his arrival, Slater heard about a businessman, Moses Brown, who wanted to start a textile mill. He sent Brown a letter saying,

> Sir,—A few days ago I was informed that you wanted a manager of cotton spinning, . . . in which business I flatter myself that I can give the greatest satisfaction, in making machinery, making good yard, either for stockings or twist, as any that is made in England; as I have had opportunity, and oversight, of Sir Richard Arkwright's works, and in Mr. Strutt's mill upwards of eight years.[1]

Brown, who had already made an unsuccessful attempt to obtain a working spinning machine, was excited by Slater's offer. He went into business with Slater and financed the production of the first successful spinning machines in the United States. This partnership was one of the first important steps toward American industrialization.

## The Government Encourages Industry

As the 1700s came to a close, American leaders were divided in their opinions about whether or not industrialization should be encouraged. Alexander Hamilton, the nation's secretary of the treasury, believed that industrialization was vital for the United States economy to prosper. He knew that factories, with their water-powered machinery, would dramatically increase the nation's productivity.[2]

In his *Report on Manufactures*, presented to Congress in 1791, Hamilton laid out his arguments for America's industrialization. He felt that by building factories in America, the nation could achieve several goals. Industrialization would broaden the nation's economic base and attract more European immigrants—which would increase the market for America's farm products. In time, Hamilton knew, industrialization would put America on the same economic footing as the industrialized nations of

Europe. In his report, Hamilton reminded Congress that "The extreme embarrassments of the United States during the late War, from an incapacity of supplying themselves, are still a matter of keen recollection."[3]

Secretary of State Thomas Jefferson, who was later to become president, disagreed. He had visited England and witnessed the horrible conditions factory workers were forced to endure. He did not want the same thing to happen in America. Jefferson hoped that

*Alexander Hamilton, the first secretary of the treasury, was a strong supporter of American industrialization. In his* Report on Manufactures, *he presented his plan for building factories in the United States.*

instead of becoming industrialized, the United States could remain a nation of farmers and small-businesspeople. In 1785, Jefferson wrote,

> While we have land to labor then, let us never wish to see our citizens occupied at a work-bench or twirling a distaff [a staff used in spinning that holds wool, flax, or other fiber]. . . . For the general operations of manufacture, let our workshops remain in Europe. It is better to carry provisions and materials to work-men there, than bring them to the provisions and materials, and with them their manners and principals.[4]

The debate over whether the United States government should encourage industrialization or allow the nation's economy to remain mostly agricultural continued throughout the nation's first century. In the end, Hamilton's ideas won. Not only was industrialization encouraged, but a national bank was set up to help fund the creation of factories in America.

## Patent Laws Encourage Invention

In America's early years as an independent nation, no laws had yet been passed to guarantee an inventor's right to own and control his work. Once an idea or machine had been given public exposure, anyone was free to copy and use it. So in 1790, Congress passed the first United States patent law. It gave sole control over an article or process to its inventor for seventeen years. This encouraged many talented people to spend their time and money creating inventions they could market to the business community with hopes of making a profit.

Soon after the law was passed, the first patent office was set up in New York City. During its first decade of operation, the United States Patent Office issued patents for only 276 new inventions. Later on, as more people saw that there was a profit to be made in designing useful inventions, this number increased tremendously.

Although many of the basic ideas that started the Industrial Revolution came from England, American inventors were soon able to improve upon them. They studied the British machines and came up with ways to make them operate quicker and more efficiently. Because of this, America soon became known around the world as a nation of innovators—people who could improve on existing products.

## Eli Whitney's Contributions

Eli Whitney, an American inventor who lived in Connecticut, played a very important role in the Industrial Revolution. In 1793, he invented the cotton gin, a machine that revolutionized the way cotton was processed. Previously, it took a person a full day to separate seeds from one pound of cotton by hand. A cotton gin could do the job fifty times as fast.

Before the industrialization of the textile industry, there was no real need for the cotton gin. More cotton was available than home spinners and weavers could use. Other fibers such as flax and wool were also available. Now that fiber could rapidly be transformed into cloth, however, cotton and other raw fibers were in great demand. Because of the cotton gin, cotton became a valuable crop in the South.

By 1840, Southern plantations were producing over 60 percent of the world's cotton supply. After textile mills in the United States had all the cotton they could use, cotton became an important export. In the mid-1800s, the sale of cotton to England and other countries amounted to about two thirds of all American exports.[5]

Another of Eli Whitney's contributions to the Industrial Revolution came from his work with guns. In the late 1700s, all firearms were crafted by gunsmiths, who made each part by hand. If a gun broke, a new piece had to be designed to match it.

Eli Whitney had a better idea. He realized that if the parts used to make guns were interchangeable, it would be easier and less expensive to replace them when they broke. On May 1, 1798, Whitney wrote a letter to Secretary of the Treasury Hamilton to obtain the money he needed to put his idea into practice. In his letter, Whitney said:

> I have a number of workmen and apprentices whom I have instructed in working Wood and Metals. . . . I should like to undertake to manufacture ten or Fifteen Thousand Stand of Arms.
>
> I am persuaded that Machinery moved by water adapted to this Business would greatly diminish the labor and facilitate the Manufacture of this Article. Machines for forging, rolling, boreing, Grinding, Polishing etc. may all be used to advantage.[6]

*In 1793, Eli Whitney invented the cotton gin, which could separate the seeds from cotton fifty times as fast as a person working by hand.*

At the time of Whitney's request, the United States government was concerned that the army might not have sufficient weapons if a war broke out. So even though they had doubts about whether Whitney could really produce as many guns as he proposed, they decided to fund the project.

A little over two years later, Whitney went to Washington, D.C., with a box that contained the parts needed to assemble ten guns. He presented the box to President Thomas Jefferson and a group of Cabinet officials. Then he asked them to assemble the guns from a group of identical parts. By the time the demonstration was over, all ten guns had been assembled and fired.

This marked the beginning of mass production—making large quantities of identical goods—in America.

# THE FACTORY SYSTEM

In the early 1800s, most Americans farmed or ran small businesses. They had heard about factories in Europe, where goods were mass-produced on a scale they could hardly imagine. They had heard about the long days that people who operated these machines had to work and about the sickness that often resulted from unhealthy working conditions. But few Americans living at that time could have imagined how quickly industrialization would come to their own nation and, within less than a century, completely change the economy.

## Textile Factories in Lowell, Massachusetts

In 1813, a group of wealthy Boston businessmen set up a textile factory in Lowell, Massachusetts, called the Merrimack Manufacturing Company. Most of their employees were New England farm girls between the ages of sixteen and thirty who wanted the opportunity to earn some money of their own before they got married and started a family. Depending on how well they performed their assigned tasks, they were paid from $2.40 to $3.40 per week.

That was only about half of what men received for textile work. However, it was far better than the dollar a week or less a woman could make by working as a domestic servant or seamstress. So, for the first time in American history, women became serious wage earners. Instead of having to turn over their money to help support the family, as they had in the past, these women had money of their own to spend on things they wanted to buy. One mill girl from a New Hampshire farm wrote home to her sister:

> Since I have wrote you, another pay day has come around. I earned 14 dollars and a half, nine and a half dollars besides my board. The folks think I get along just first-rate, they say. I like it as well as ever . . . The thought that I am living on no one is a happy one indeed.[1]

Working in the Lowell factories presented many new opportunities that were not available to girls on the farm. During their free time, mill girls were encouraged to take classes, attend lectures, and borrow books from the local library. Almost overnight, a business district grew up around the mills. When author Charles Dickens visited Lowell, he marveled, "One would swear that every kind of 'Bakery,' 'Grocery,' and 'Bookbindery' and every other kind of store, took its shutters down for the first time, and started in business yesterday."[2]

Once they had tasted city life, many of the mill girls were reluctant to return to the drudgery of life at home. When Sally Rice's parents wrote to her, asking that she leave the Lowell mills and return to the family farm in Vermont, she replied, "I must . . . have something of my own before many more years have passed. And where is that something coming from if I go home and earn nothing?"[3]

While the Lowell mill girls were experiencing their first taste of independence, they still had to deal with the many regulations set up by factory owners. Working conditions were not always ideal. Factories were hot and poorly ventilated, and the girls were allowed few breaks. In addition to work rules, company-owned boardinghouses had their own sets of rules. A 10:00 P.M. curfew was enforced, and mill girls were only allowed to have male visitors if a chaperone was present. The girls were also required to attend church services. If a mill girl refused to obey any of the company rules, she was in danger of being fired and sent back home. But despite all the regulations and working conditions that were harsh and often monotonous, the Lowell mill girls had a much better life than workers in most other English and American mills at the time.

The Merrimack Manufacturing Company made enormous profits with its mills. Within three decades, Lowell was transformed from a farm community into a growing city with a population of thirty thousand.[4]

This success prompted many other wealthy businessmen to invest in textile mills. The cloth industry grew rapidly in the early 1800s. Production went from one hundred thirty thousand spindles in 1815 to nearly a million by 1825. Mill towns could soon be found in the Southern states as well as along the rivers of New England.

Other occupations were also being transformed by industrialization. One of these crafts was shoe making. Although some steps still had to be performed by hand, machines that could sew leather, nail on heels, and perform other tasks much quicker than a cobbler could do by hand were coming into use. The quality of mass-produced shoes was not as good as those made by hand, but the low price attracted many buyers.

At first, most factories in the United States were powered by water. Rivers and streams were plentiful in America. Once the water-powered equipment was bought and put into place, it cost almost nothing to run. But by the mid-1800s, steam engines, which were powered by burning coal, came into general use. This led to an increased demand for coal, and it greatly expanded the mining industry in America.

## A Changing Workforce

One of the biggest problems American factory owners faced was finding a steady supply of workers to operate their machines. Unlike Europe, the United States had plenty of inexpensive farmland. Even though the profit one could earn by farming was not always dependable, many people preferred to work their own soil instead of putting in long hours in someone else's factory.

To fill their job openings, many factory owners advertised for workers in Europe. They sent agents overseas who told Europeans about the good jobs available in America. Many people in Europe were poor and in need of work. When news of good jobs in the United States spread, thousands were willing to leave their homeland and travel to American cities to start a new life.

Coming to America was a dream for many Europeans. They saw it as the only way to improve their lives. In America, they had heard, they would have a chance to earn more money, eat better food, and have a better place to live than they did back home. Even though the working conditions in American factories were harsh by today's standards, the life the immigrants found here was generally better than what they had endured in Europe.

One European immigrant to America wrote a letter back home to his family saying, "Tell Miriam there is no sending children to bed without their supper, or husbands to work without dinner in their bags [in America]."[5]

The 1860 census revealed that 1.6 million Irish, 1.3 million German, and 588,000 British immigrants were living and working in America. A large percentage of those immigrants worked in factories and mills. Even those who did not fully understand the English language had no trouble performing the repetitive tasks that factory work required.

But once factory owners had enough immigrant labor, the living and working conditions they provided for their employees quickly declined. Once their needs for workers had been met, employers no longer needed to use good conditions to advertise the jobs they had available. Employers also discovered that many immigrants, who had been accustomed to poverty in Europe, would work for less money than native-born Americans and rarely dared to complain for fear of losing their jobs.

Most immigrant families could afford only a small apartment in a tenement house located near the factory that employed them. Sometimes over a hundred

*As the factory system became more popular and profitable, workers looking for jobs crowded into the cities. Because of the high cost of land in the city, houses were often crowded together, like these in Pittsburgh, Pennsylvania.*

people lived in a two-story or three-story house that was originally designed to accommodate one family comfortably.

## Factory Conditions

Working conditions in American factories during the 1800s were generally unhealthy. Many factories had poor ventilation, and pollution of all kinds filled the air. Textile workers, for example, often became ill from inhaling the dust produced by spinning thread and weaving cloth.

As with the factories and mills in England, American supervisors insisted that their employees work long hours and enforced rigid work schedules. People who had come from farms were used to working by the cycle of the seasons. But being employed by a factory meant working by a time clock and being told when to start, stop, and take a break.

Once factory owners had a good supply of people looking for jobs, working conditions became harsher. Before long, the lives of many factory workers in America were no better than those of their counterparts in England. In fact, the average factory worker had little more free time than the slaves who labored on Southern plantations.

These and other complaints against factory owners led to the formation of trade labor unions. A few unions were formed in the 1830s, and the movement quickly gained momentum. By the 1850s, many trades had organized unions, and strikes were common throughout the country. Unions gave workers something they never had before—the bargaining power that came with being able to express their grievances against factory owners as a group.

In 1860, the shoemakers' union went on strike in parts of New England. Nearly twenty thousand workers in two dozen towns in Massachusetts, Maine, and New Hampshire were involved in the strike. Within a few weeks, the workers' demands for better wages were met and they went back to work.[6]

During the mid-1860s, a group of labor unions joined to form the National Labor Union (NLU). The NLU's main objectives were to campaign for fair wages and eight-hour workdays. A banner the NLU raised during their rallies proclaimed, "Eight hours for work; eight hours for rest; eight hours for what we will!"[7] By the early 1870s, the NLU had attracted over six hundred thousand members, making the union a force to be reckoned with.

Other workers' unions were also formed during this period. The Knights of Labor, formed in 1869, started as a secret organization of garment cutters who worked in Philadelphia mills. A decade later, the organization's leader, Terence V. Powderly, decided it was time for the union to expand.

Powderly wanted the Knights of Labor to include people of all trades, racial backgrounds, religions, and skill levels. He wanted it to become "one big union" for the "toiling millions."[8] Powderly's plan was successful. By 1886, the Knights of Labor had over seven hundred thousand members.

As unions gained members and power, strikes became more and more common. In 1885, when the

Missouri Pacific announced pay cuts for their workers, the Knights of Labor held a strike against the railroad. The governors of Missouri and Kansas helped to mediate the situation. In the end, not only were the railroad workers' wages restored, but the Missouri Pacific promised to pay them at a rate of time and a half when they were required to work overtime. The success of this strike led to many others.

But strikes did not always produce the results the unions wanted. In several instances, violence erupted and many people were injured or killed before the strike was settled.

The railroad strikes that took place in 1877 after workers' wages were lowered were the largest and most violent of the century. The strikes started in Baltimore, Maryland, then spread across the nation. Trains were stopped and railroad property was destroyed. By the time federal troops put an end to the strike, nearly one hundred people had been killed in the riots.

At the time, few laws concerning working conditions and hours had been passed. Those that did exist were rarely enforced. Even children were forced to work long hours. In 1870, approximately seven hundred thousand children were working twelve- to sixteen-hour days in factories and mills. Despite the long hours, they received only $2.50 per week for their labor.[9]

## City Life

Throughout the 1880s, the population of America's cities grew steadily. During the last half of the century, agricultural machinery had come into such wide use that fewer farm laborers were needed than ever before. So people whose families had farmed the land for many generations decided to move to cities and try to find work in factories. European immigrants also added substantially to the increasing population of the cities.

Large cities such as New York and Philadelphia soon grew to the point that few people could live within walking distance of the factory that employed them. As a result, public transportation came into being. Horse-drawn buses, known as omnibuses, were popular with city-dwellers. By 1835, about a hundred omnibuses were in use in New York City alone.

Even at that early date, traffic had become a problem. In an 1835 issue of the *New York Journal of Commerce*, a writer described the situation by saying,

> The character of the omnibus driver has become brutal and dangerous in the highest degree. They race up and down Broadway with the utmost fury, committing scenes of outrage, in which the lives of citizens riding in light [weight] vehicles are put in imminent hazard.[10]

*As many people moved from the country to the cities to work in factories, transportation had to be provided for them. Before the automobile, horse-drawn wagons and omnibuses, like those seen here in Chicago, were popular modes of transportation.*

City life was different from life on the farm in almost every way. Some people who moved to the city were glad they made the change. But others soon became disappointed at the harsh realities of urban living.[11] Many of the city's brightest attractions were far too expensive for most newcomers' budgets. They could only gaze at the fine theaters, expensive homes, private schools, stores with fancy goods, and other things that were available only to those who could afford them.

Even for people of limited means, however, living in the city had advantages. Libraries were available where people of any income level could borrow books. Public schools had opened in many American cities and towns. Churches and synagogues of many denominations sprang up to serve the diverse population.

City-dwellers could also select from a wide variety of goods. Soon after the Civil War was over, canned and packaged foods that had been manufactured during the war only for the military were made available to the public. Ready-made clothes for men, women, and children also became available in many parts of the country.

The way consumer goods were sold to the public was also changing. People in rural areas often depended on a general store that had a little bit of everything. But in the city, many merchants decided to specialize, selling only one type of product, such as clothes, food, or tools. These big-city specialty stores, made possible by the many products of the Industrial Revolution, were the forerunners of a trend that would soon spread across the nation.

Industry in the United States grew steadily throughout the 1800s. Factories all over the nation turned out more products than they ever had in the past. But as industries grew, so did the need for better and cheaper transportation.

# ROADS, BOATS, AND RAILROADS

## Overland Roads

In the early 1800s, most American roads were very primitive. Many were little more than a muddy path through the forest. While these had met the transportation needs of preindustrial times, they were inadequate for transporting large quantities of goods.

For example, in 1813 it took about two and a half months for a horse-drawn wagon to take a load of cotton from Massachusetts to South Carolina. At that time, a ton of goods could be shipped from Europe to the United States for nine dollars. In America, goods could be moved only thirty miles overland by wagon for the same price.[1] Factory owners clearly needed faster finished products from one place to another.

In 1806, Congress passed a bill that created the first National Road. The road was planned to run between Cumberland, Maryland, and the Ohio River at Wheeling in what is now West Virginia. It cost about thirteen thousand dollars a mile to build. The project was later extended through Ohio and Indiana. The National Road ended in Vandalia, Illinois, when the project was finally terminated in 1852. The total cost of the 591-mile road was just under $7 million.

The National Road was soon filled with horse-drawn wagons pulling goods to distant markets. As a result, loads of farm products and factory goods reached buyers who would otherwise not have had access to them due to the high cost of overland transportation.

The National Road was of great economic importance to the surrounding areas. Cities and towns grew up all along its path. It hastened the settlement of America's western regions.

But even after the National Road had been completed, the United States was still in desperate need of good overland transportation. President James Madison was very concerned about the problem. He knew that a better system of roads was very important to the United States' economy. Good roads were also needed for military use and for faster mail delivery.

President Madison believed that the federal government should play a role in financing and building these roads to connect cities and towns across the nation. In December 1815, during his annual address to Congress, Madison told Congress of "the great importance of establishing throughout our country the roads and canals that can best be executed under national authority."[2] He asked Congress to pass a bill appropriating the money as soon as possible so improvements to the nation's roads could be made.

Even though nearly everyone acknowledged that better roads were important to the nation's future, some lawmakers felt that federal money should not be used for such projects.[3] The debate over whether Congress should be allowed to build and improve a national system of roads went on for decades.

Meanwhile, state and industrial leaders were looking for other alternatives to the transportation dilemma. Throughout the eastern and mid-Atlantic states, turnpikes, also known as toll roads, were built with state and private funds. Many of the nation's early turnpike projects were financed for under one hundred thousand dollars.[4] Anyone who had money to invest could contact the turnpike corporation and purchase turnpike stocks. State governments also contributed to the construction funds. However, the bulk of turnpike stocks was usually owned by wealthy businessmen.

They were often the same merchants and factory owners who had led the push for roads to be built to improve transportation of their products.

Few turnpikes lived up to people's hopes and expectations. They were more expensive to build and operate than their engineers had imagined. Businessmen were disappointed at the high cost of using the roads. The tolls collected from their use rarely made a profit for the corporations that financed them. Out of the two hundred thirty turnpikes built in New England, fewer than ten made enough profit to pay adequate returns to their investors.[5]

## Steamboats

During the 1800s, riverboats were one of the least expensive ways for industries to move their products over long distances. Goods were loaded onto flatboats and floated downstream. Whereas it was relatively easy to transport goods downstream, it was nearly impossible to use the river to transport goods upstream against the current. This created problems for Southern businesses that wanted to market their goods to cities in the North.

But inventors were working on ideas that would change all that. The idea of powering boats with steam engines was first explored in the late 1700s. At that time, a few small steamboats provided passenger service on New England rivers.

The first American steamboat to provide passenger service regularly was invented and operated by John Fitch. Fitch saw a bright future for steam-powered boats. He sent letters to Congress and to many of the nation's leaders, describing his vision of the steamboat's future.

His letter to Benjamin Franklin said, "It is a matter of great magnitude not only to the United States but to every maritime power in the world. . . . It will answer [be useful] for sea voyages as well as for inland navigation."[6] But when government officials refused to back his idea, Fitch looked to private investors for the funds he needed. Fitch's steamboat could move along at eight miles an hour. In 1790, Fitch provided passenger service between Philadelphia, Pennsylvania, and Trenton, New Jersey. The cost of the forty-mile trip was about $1.25.

During the summer of 1790, Fitch's steamboat made over thirty trips between the two cities. The boat's steam-powered engines operated successfully, but few people were willing to ride on such an unusual vehicle. Many were afraid that the powerful steam engine would explode. With every trip, the venture lost money. Eventually, the people who had invested in the project withdrew their support.[7]

Other passenger steamboats were built and put into service during this period. But none of them became commercially successful.

Then Robert Fulton, an artist and mechanic who lived in Pennsylvania, took the ideas used by the early steamboat inventors and improved upon them. He believed that if a steamboat could be made large enough and powerful enough, it could be used to transport not only people but also raw materials and products. Fulton worked with the famous silversmith and Revolutionary War hero, Paul Revere, who provided the sheets of copper Fulton needed to make the huge boiler that would power such a steamboat.

Finally, in 1807, Fulton's steamboat, the *Clermont*, was complete. It was three times larger than any other steamboat that had been built. That year, Fulton showed for the first time what a steam-powered boat could do. The *Clermont*'s powerful engines pushed it up the Hudson River from New York City to Albany, New York. With its steam-driven paddle wheels, the *Clermont* made the 150-mile trip at five miles per hour. Although slow by today's standards, the *Clermont* moved goods much faster than goods moved on flatboats or over land.

Before the age of steamboats, it took about three months to travel from New Orleans, Louisiana, to Louisville, Kentucky. On a steamboat, the trip could

THE WHOLE COUNTRY TALKED OF NOTHING BUT THE SEA MONSTER BELCHING FORTH FIRE AND SMOKE. THE FISHERMEN BECAME TERRIFIED AND ROWED HOMEWARDS, AND THEY SAW NOTHING BUT DESTRUCTION DEVASTATING THEIR FISHING GROUNDS, WHILE THE WREATHS OF BLACK VAPOR . . . PRODUCED GREAT EXCITEMENT AMONG THE BOATMEN . . . FROM THAT TIME, ROBERT FULTON, ESQ., BECAME KNOWN AND RESPECTED AS THE AUTHOR AND BUILDER OF THE FIRST STEAM PACKET FROM WHICH WE PLAINLY SEE THE RAPID IMPROVEMENT IN COMMERCE AND CIVILIZATION.[8]

*This excerpt is from the account of an observer who witnessed the first voyage of the* Clermont *on August 7, 1807.*

be made in a little over a week. This cut the cost of transporting goods upstream by about 90 percent.[9] Within a few years, steamboats were regularly traveling up and down the rivers of the East Coast. Within a decade, they could be seen as far west as the Mississippi River. Zadok Cramer, author of a boat pilot's manual called *The Navigator*, wrote in the 1811 edition of his book,

> There is now on foot a new method of navigating our western waters, particularly the Ohio and the Mississippi rivers. This is with boats propelled by the power of steam . . . It will be a novel sight, and as pleasing as novel, to see a huge boat work her way up the windings of the Ohio, without the appearance of sail, oar, pole, or any manual labor about her.[10]

Some steamboats were used mostly for transporting goods; others were designed with fancy accommodations that rivaled the best hotels. These steamboats were designed to attract the business of well-to-do travelers. In 1866, the first of these great steamboats, the *Ruth*, was introduced. The *Ruth* had four decks and could comfortably carry more than a thousand passengers in style—as well as 250 tons of cotton, tobacco, hay, and other freight. The *Ruth*, with her 268-foot-long dining room and fancy murals painted on her walls, was a magnificent ship. She was quickly dubbed the "Wonder of the West" by a New Orleans newspaper.[11]

Oceangoing steamboats also became common in the 1800s. As early as 1829, steamboats were regularly traveling from New York to London. Most of these early steamships carried passengers as well as mail, packages, and light freight.

Once investors saw that steamship transportation could be profitable, they were eager to put their money into such ventures. But in the rush to produce bigger, better, and faster steamboats, some designers did not

*After the pioneering voyage of the* Clermont, *steamboats became a popular means of travel. Here, the St. Louis waterfront is shown crowded with steamboats.*

make sure their ships were safely constructed. Accidents, especially boiler explosions that threw large quantities of boiling water and hot steam into the air, were fairly common. By 1850, nearly one hundred fifty boiler explosions had been recorded, resulting in the death of at least fourteen hundred people. By then, approximately one out of three Mississippi steamboats had been lost in accidents.[12] But despite the dangers involved with this kind of transportation, there was still a big demand for steamboats and their services.

## Canals Connect the Nation's Rivers

Even after steamboats had become a common sight in America, the problem of river transportation had not been totally solved. Rivers could only carry goods within their limited boundaries. Many valuable natural resources were still cut off from the factories that could use them. A United States Senate committee report written in 1816 highlighted the problem. It said, "A coal mine may exist in the United States not more than ten miles from valuable ores of iron and other materials, and both of them be useless unless a canal is established between them, as the price of land carriage is too great to be borne by either."[13] So engineers went to work to find ways of connecting the nation's great rivers by building canals.

The Erie Canal, which connected the waterways of Albany and Buffalo, New York, was the first of these great undertakings. The proposed canal was to be 364 miles long. Large amounts of money had to be raised in order to build it. And it would take the nation's best engineers years to figure out how to construct it.

While there were many drawbacks to such a large and risky undertaking, there were some who believed the idea could work. Among them was the mayor of New York, DeWitt Clinton. He served on a commission to study the feasibility of a canal and helped map out a possible route for it. An 1815 petition in favor of the canal stated,

> As an organ of communication between the Hudson, the Mississippi, the St. Lawrence and the great lakes of the north and west and their tributary rivers, it [the Erie Canal] will create the greatest inland trade ever witnessed. The most fertile and extensive regions of America will avail themselves of its facilities for a market.[14]

Two years later, a bill to create a canal fund was passed in the New York legislature. It was estimated that the project would cost $7 million. This money was to be raised over a twenty-five-year period. The project officially started on July 4, 1817, in Rome, New York. In 1825, the entire length of the canal was opened.

*As businesses realized the benefits of canals as a means of transporting goods to far-off markets, more and more canals were built. This map shows the rapid growth of a system of canals in the mid-nineteenth century.*

Industries were quick to take advantage of the new opportunities the canal presented. They could reach new markets with their goods. Materials could be transported at a fraction of the previous cost. Before the Erie Canal was built, it cost about $125 to transport a ton of goods from New York City to Buffalo, New York, by wagon. The same goods could be taken through the canal for only $5. Passenger boats also made heavy use of the new waterway.

The Erie Canal was a great success. In its first year of operation, at least 13,100 boats went through the nation's first artificial waterway, earning New York State $556,000 in tolls. This news prompted other states to finance the building of their own canals. For example, in 1825, Pennsylvania started building a canal that connected the Delaware River to the Ohio. In the decades that followed, canals were built that connected many of the nation's important waterways. By 1840, more than 3,326 miles of man-made canals were in use.[15]

## Railroads

Factory owners were still looking for other ways to transport their goods. Steam-powered trains proved to be an alternative. Railroads had the advantage of being able to move goods over land much cheaper, and at a much faster pace, than horse-drawn wagons. Railroads were also able to move goods twice as fast as steamboats.[16]

A few small railroad lines had been built in parts of New England as early as the 1830s, mostly to transport goods between factories and canals. These railroads, which were financed by industry as well as by local and state governments, soon proved to be financially successful. But at the time, not much private money was available to finance the building of large railroad lines.

So industrialists and others who had an interest in the project took the matter to Congress. They argued that if the government were to help finance the railroads, it would serve not only the needs of industry but also the needs of the United States military. It would also speed up postal delivery and provide a new form of private transportation.

After debating the issue, Congress agreed that a system of railroads was necessary for the nation's economic well-being. During the 1850s and 1860s, the United States government loaned railroad companies $65 million and gave them 131 million acres of land on which to construct railroad tracks.[17]

In the years that followed, railroad construction took off at a feverish pace. Construction gangs, many of whom were Irish immigrants, laid rails for the Union Pacific Railroad westward from Nebraska.

Some people feared the changes that the railroad would bring to their community, and tried to stop the spread of the railroads. This poster was circulated around Philadelphia, Pennsylvania, in 1839.

Nearly ten thousand Chinese immigrant workers employed by the Central Pacific Railroad laid rails from San Francisco, California, toward the East.

America's first coast-to-coast railroad became a reality when the two lines met at Promontory Point, Utah, on May 10, 1869. Now that the East and the West were linked by railroad lines, industry could expand into many new markets. Areas that were once isolated could begin to feel the benefits of the Industrial Revolution.

While the need for better transportation was being met, another need of the industrial age was also being addressed by American inventors. It was the need for better and faster communication.

Until the mid-1800s, communication between cities was very slow. It took days or even weeks for a letter or package to reach its destination. It again took that long to receive an answer. This held back the speed at which business could be done. But inventors were already working on projects that would change everything. New electronic means of communication were being developed that could transport messages from one place to another instantaneously.

# NEW WAYS TO COMMUNICATE

## Samuel Morse and the Telegraph

Samuel Morse, the inventor of the telegraph, became interested in electricity in the 1830s. At one point in his work, he asked himself, "If the presence of electricity can be made visible in any part of the circuit, I see no reason why intelligence may not be transmitted instantaneously by electricity."[1] He was surprised that no one had come up with the idea before him.

Morse immediately went to work developing the telegraph—a system of opening and closing an electrical connection to send a message. He also developed Morse Code—an alphabet of long and short bursts of electricity that stood for letters and numbers. The telegraph operator at the receiving end could interpret these clicks to translate the message, then pass it along to the person to whom it had been sent.

But before any of that could happen, Morse had to acquire a patent for his telegraph and obtain government funding to continue his work. A long struggle with the United States government began to prove the worthiness of his invention.

On September 27, 1837, Morse wrote a letter to Levi Woodlawn, the secretary of the treasury. In his letter, he laid out his proposal and explained the many advantages of having a system of electric telegraph stations set up across the nation.

After many delays, the United States government appropriated money for Morse to continue his experiments. In 1843, the "Morse Bill" passed through Congress by a margin of only six votes. With part of the funding, Morse was able to set up an experimental telegraph line between Washington, D.C., and Baltimore. On May 24, 1844, he sent the first telegraph message, "What hath God wrought!" over the forty-mile line.[2]

Telegraph wires and offices soon sprang up all over the country. By 1861, the Western Union Company had installed a total of seventy-six thousand miles of telegraph lines. Many of these lines were strung alongside railroad tracks.

Once the telegraph was in service, businessmen as well as private individuals could communicate at speeds they never dreamed possible. Whereas letters in the past could only move as fast as a horse or ship, telegraph messages flew over the wires instantaneously. No longer did it take weeks to communicate with people in a distant city. Often, telegraph messages were sent, transcribed, and delivered all in the same day.

An article that appeared in a July 1883 issue of *Harper's Weekly* said,

> The function of the telegraph in our highly organized commercial and social life has come to be as general and important as that of the mail. In some respects, it is even more of a necessity. . . . Not only is it an indisputable instrument of ordinary exchanges, but it is absolutely necessary for the safe administration of the railways themselves.[3]

This new, rapid means of communication had a remarkable effect on business. Now factory owners could quickly find out which raw materials were available from distant factories. They could compare the rates different rail lines charged for transportation.

Orders could often be shipped on the same day they were requested.

The United States government also benefited from the establishment of telegraph lines across the nation. Military orders, which once had to be delivered by a rider on horseback, could now be transmitted instantaneously with the telegraph. Politicians in Washington could better keep in touch with the people in the state they represented.

As wonderful as the telegraph was, though, people still could not hear each other's voices. Another problem was the lack of privacy. To send a telegram, one had to go through a telegraph operator and tell him or her the message one wanted to send. Then the sender had to wait until the other party received it and replied in order to get the answer.

## Alexander Graham Bell and the Telephone

In the late 1800s, many inventors were trying to find a way to electrically transmit the human voice over wires. It was a Scottish immigrant, Alexander Graham Bell, and his partner, Thomas Watson, who eventually developed the idea into a commercial success. In 1875, Bell stated, "If I can get a mechanism which will make a current of electricity vary in intensity, as air varies in density when sound is passing through it, I can telegraph any sound, even the sound of speech."[4]

A year later, Bell spoke the very first words over a telephone: "Mr. Watson, come here—I want you."[5] The experiment proved that human voices could indeed be transmitted over a wire. Several months later, at the age of twenty-nine, Bell was able to get a patent for his invention.

In 1877, Bell started the Bell Telephone Company. In 1884, he opened the first long-distance line, which connected telephones in New York and Boston. At that time, long-distance service was very expensive. But to many businessmen, it was worth the cost to be able to

*Alexander Graham Bell astonished the American people with his invention of the telephone.*

pick up the phone and talk directly with a person or company with whom they hoped to make a deal.

In the early years of the telephone industry, all phone calls had to be placed by an operator. At first, the phone companies tried hiring boys in their late teens, but that turned out to be a disaster. The boys did not have the patience to deal with the equipment's flaws. When the supervisor was not watching, they often roughhoused and swore at customers.

A visitor to a Chicago phone office in the late 1800s said, "The racket is almost deafening. Boys are rushing madly hither and thither, while others are putting in or taking out pegs from a central framework as if they were lunatics engaged in a game of fox and geese."[6]

The phone companies soon decided to replace the rowdy boys with women, whom they felt would be calmer and have better manners.[7] In 1878, Emma M. Nutt was hired by New England Bell as the first female telephone operator. Within a few years, nearly all operators employed by telephone companies were women.

The telephone industry quickly created jobs for thousands of people across the nation. By 1890, nineteen thousand telephone operators were employed by phone companies to handle calls. Thousands more people were employed to manufacture telephones, string telephone wire, and repair broken telephones.

By 1900, nearly a million telephones were in use in America. The company Bell founded had grown tremendously. It owned one hundred local telephone companies across the country and handled over 2 billion calls a year.

Soon, telephones were considered to be more of a necessity than a luxury. This was especially true for people who ran businesses. An advertisement run by Illinois Bell Telephone Company in 1925 stated that its new, improved long-distance service offered "The kind of speed every businessman will appreciate, and can use to increase volume of sales, reduce selling expenses, expedite deliveries, obtain last minute orders, and keep in close touch with the needs of his customers."[8]

In addition to business use, telephones were installed in many private homes during the late 1800s and early 1900s. An advertising circular that was released in New Haven, Connecticut, in 1876 encouraged all men who could afford it to invest in telephone service for their homes. The ad stated, "Your wife may order your dinner, a hack [horse-drawn cab], your family physician, etc., all by Telephone without leaving the home or trusting servants to do it."[9]

Home telephones were often used for talking to friends and relatives and making arrangements for parties and family gatherings. At first, only the wealthy and upper middle class could afford to have a home phone. But as the popularity of telephones increased, the price of the service gradually fell to the point where nearly everyone could afford it.

## Thomas Edison's Inventions

Thomas Edison, who came to be known as the Wizard of Menlo Park, was one of the most prolific inventors of the 1800s. During his lifetime, he patented over a thousand inventions—including the light bulb, the automatic telegraph, and the phonograph (record player). Edison first became interested in what electricity could do when he worked as a telegraph operator for Western Union.

Edison believed that if he gathered enough talented minds in a laboratory, they could produce inventions on a regular basis.[10] He put this idea into action in 1876 when he set up his first laboratory in Menlo Park, New Jersey, with the goal of producing a new invention every ten days. This lab, located about twenty-five miles from New York City, was the world's first industrial research laboratory.

In addition to all of his inventions, Edison wanted to set up a system that could deliver electrical power to business, home, and government users. So he went to work to develop a method of generating large amounts of electricity and sending it over wires to users throughout the city.

Edison explained the advantages of electrical lights this way:

> No match is needed to light it. . . . There is neither a blaze or a flame. There is no singing nor flickering . . . it will be whiter and steadier than any known light . . . it will give no fumes or smoke. . . . The wind can't blow it out. There can be no gas explosions, and no one will suffocate because the electricity is turned on. . . . A person may have lamps made with flexible cords, and carry them from one point to another.[11]

In the late 1870s, he attempted to prove the value of electric lighting by holding public demonstrations. At first, they all ended in failure when the electric light bulbs burned out prematurely. Still, Edison continued his work.

Just after the election of President James Garfield in 1880, Edison held another demonstration. He flipped a switch that lit a string of a new type of electric lamps that were draped around his house. Spectators were astonished when, this time, the lamps stayed lit. This and other demonstrations won Edison the financial backing he needed to continue his work.

THE DAY WAS—LET ME SEE—OCTOBER 21, 1879. WE SAT AND LOOKED AND THE LAMP CONTINUED TO BURN AND THE LONGER IT BURNED THE MORE FASCINATED WE WERE. NONE OF US COULD GO TO BED AND THERE WAS NO SLEEP FOR OVER 40 HOURS; WE SAT AND JUST WATCHED IT WITH ANXIETY GROWING INTO ELATION. IT LASTED ABOUT 45 HOURS AND THEN I SAID, "IF IT WILL BURN 40 HOURS NOW I KNOW I CAN MAKE IT BURN A HUNDRED."[12]

*This is how Thomas Edison described the success of his experiments with the electric light bulb.*

At 3:00 P.M. on September 4, 1882, Edison demonstrated his lamps for the first time in New York City. J. P. Morgan and *The New York Times* were among the first to have their offices lit by electricity. The next day, a *New York Times* reporter commented, "It was not until about 7 o'clock, when it began to be dark, that the electric light really made itself known and showed how bright and steady it was. . . . Soft, mellow, grateful to the eye; it seemed most like writing by daylight."[13]

His great success won Edison the continued support of investors such as the banking firm of Drexel, Morgan and Company. They provided him with funds to help him reach his goal of building electrical power plants throughout the country.

Edison's success bred more success and added to his public image. As one Edison biographer wrote, "Between 1878 and 1882, Edison constructed the prototype for the entire electric light and power industry. . . . Edison threw open the door through which not only he but a host of scientists rushed to make discovery after discovery."[14]

## The Many Uses of Electricity

Electrical lighting in homes and offices drastically changed the way people lived. Before electricity was available, people had to do nearly all of their work in the daytime. Kerosene lamps and candles were available, but they were expensive to burn for long periods. Once electric lights were installed in homes, businesses, and on street corners, everything changed. Normal daytime activities could continue long after the sun had disappeared below the horizon.

People all over America were thrilled to see electric power light up their towns. An article published in the November 20, 1886, issue of the *Huntington Advertiser Weekly* described the reaction of people in

*People were thrilled as electric lights were set up in their cities and towns. This postcard shows a street scene in Columbus, Ohio, shortly after the installation of electric lighting.*

Huntington, West Virginia, when electric lights first lit up the dark skies of their city:

> The evening was dark and wet, and the pedestrians . . . picking their way over crossings . . . hailed with joy the sudden flash of fifteen globes of electric fire, having light equal to the power of the light of thirty thousand candles. . . . With electric lights, water works [plumbing] assured, and the finest opera house in the state, all we need to rival New York in dignity and importance is an elevated railway and a (crooked) alderman [city councilman].[15]

Once electric power was widely available in private homes, industrial leaders sought inventors to create a whole new type of consumer goods that required electrical power to operate. These included electrically powered washing machines, ovens, sewing machines, and so on.

Many of the factories that turned out these goods were themselves powered by electricity. Electricity had advantages over steam as a power source for manufacturing. Electrically powered factories could be set up almost anywhere. By the end of the century, electricity had replaced steam as a power source for industry.

# THE AGE OF BIG BUSINESS

During the first half of the 1800s, most factories were relatively small. They marketed their goods only to the people who lived nearby. Improvements in transportation in the mid- to late 1800s made it possible for businessmen to ship goods to distant markets. To serve these larger markets, factories expanded. Equipment was installed that was able to produce larger quantities of goods. This was the beginning of the age of big business.

## Combinations and Mergers

The expansion of factories and other businesses into new markets had wide-ranging effects. Companies that once had an area all to themselves now competed with other businesses offering similar products. As a result of this competition, companies often had to lower their prices to hold on to their customers. Many businesses were not able to survive these endless rounds of price-cutting and were forced to close.

The salt industry in Michigan was one of the first to be affected by this new industrial trend. In the 1860s, the endless price war was driving many salt companies out of business. So the owners of the Michigan salt companies got together and discussed the matter. In 1869, they formed the Michigan Salt Association. The salt-company owners agreed to divide up their service areas and customers. They then set the price for salt at twice what it had been before.[1]

The Michigan Salt Association was the first organization set up to prevent price wars and other forms of competition between businesses that offered similar products or services. Other industries soon followed. Within a few decades, the railroads, whiskey industry, and many other service and manufacturing businesses had worked out similar deals with their competitors that kept prices high and competition low. But these organizations were often informal, and the business leaders involved in these groups did not always keep their word.

Some large, well-financed companies bought out their smaller rivals. Through a series of such purchases, big-business leaders were able to continually expand their production facilities and become increasingly larger. Eventually, they might be able to own all of the companies engaged in the type of business they were doing, and would have a monopoly, or trust. This was known as horizontal expansion.

Another way of controlling the market, known as vertical expansion, was to buy the businesses that furnished the raw materials, tools, and transportation necessary to manufacture a product and get it to market. Rather than owning every company engaged in the same business, the monopoly would come about because one company owned all the different types of businesses needed to compete in a certain industry. As a result, products could be produced more cheaply and easily because the company would not have to pay prices set by competitors for the various services. The company itself would be able to provide all necessary services to make its products.

The Swift meat company is one example of such vertical expansion. By the 1880s, Swift & Company controlled everything from the purchase of cattle in Chicago stockyards to the refrigerated wagons that delivered their beef products to stores across the nation. Because the same company owned everything it needed to produce and distribute its product, the middleman was eliminated. As a result, the cost of doing business could be kept lower.[2]

## Andrew Carnegie and the Steel Industry

The steel industry was one of the first to benefit from the rapid industrial expansion in this new era. Much steel was needed to build ships and trains. It was also needed to build factory machines, as well as some consumer goods.

Andrew Carnegie, an immigrant from Scotland, was one of the first Americans to profit from the steel boom. After witnessing how the Bessemer process of manufacturing steel worked in England, he rushed home to Pennsylvania to build the world's largest steel mill. It opened in 1875. During the next twenty-five years, he built several more steel mills throughout the state. Steel produced by Carnegie's mills went into the

*Andrew Carnegie was a Scottish immigrant who became a millionaire in the steel industry.*

Washington Monument, the Brooklyn Bridge, and the elevated railroad in New York City.

Carnegie took over rival steel companies when they fell on hard times. He also bought the companies that furnished the materials he needed to produce his steel, as well as the companies that transported his goods. By 1900, Andrew Carnegie's company was producing 3 million tons of steel per year. The company's annual profits were nearly $40 million.[3]

Carnegie believed that the wealthy should use some of their money to fund charitable causes and other worthy projects. He built three thousand libraries all over the United States at a cost of nearly $60 million. His other contributions to society include Carnegie Hall in New York City, and numerous endowment funds. Carnegie also spent large amounts of money to keep his steel plants running as well as possible.

Unfortunately, most of the workers who helped Carnegie earn his millions saw little reward for their efforts. The steel towns that surrounded his plants were run down more often than not. One writer of the time said, "His vision of what might be done with wealth . . . serenely overlooked the means by which wealth had been acquired."[4]

When novelist Hamlin Garland visited some of the steel towns operated by Carnegie's company, he lamented that "the streets were horrible; the buildings poor; the sidewalks sunken and full of holes. . . . Everywhere the yellow mud of the streets lay kneaded into sticky masses through which groups of pale, lean men slouched in faded garments [have to walk]."[5]

But coming from a poor family himself, Carnegie felt that anyone with real business intelligence could make his or her way to a life of wealth in America. That was one reason he built so many libraries. He believed in helping those with talent help themselves become successful. He once commented on the natural ability of certain businessmen, saying, "take away all our money, our great works, ore mines and coke ovens, but leave our organization, and in four years I shall have re-established myself."[6]

## John D. Rockefeller and Standard Oil

John D. Rockefeller, the creator of Standard Oil, headed one of the nation's first large oil businesses. He and his younger brother formed William Rockefeller & Co. of New York in 1865. One year after the first oil pipeline was laid at Pothole, Pennsylvania, the Rockefeller brothers gained control of it. The Standard Oil Company was organized in 1867.

In 1879, John D. Rockefeller organized the Standard Oil Trust. Thirty-eight oil refineries, which would process the oil, were involved in the deal. The business continued to grow through mergers until Rockefeller controlled 90 percent of the nation's oil refineries.

Through many business deals, Standard Oil came to control so much oil that it could pressure railroad lines to lower their prices for transporting its product.

Several other important industries came under the control of monopolies in the late 1800s. These included the railroad, meatpacking, tobacco, sugar, whiskey, banking, and the coal- and iron-mining industries. Powerful bankers such as J. P. Morgan often helped finance these expansions.

*John D. Rockefeller, the founder of the Standard Oil Company, eventually came to control 90 percent of the oil refineries in the United States.*

The men who built these huge companies felt that their superiority made them fit to control such large amounts of wealth and commerce. Andrew Carnegie expressed this view when he said of George Pullman, who controlled the sleeping car industry in the late 1800s, "Pullman monopolized everything. It was well that it should be so. The men had arisen who could manage, and the tools belonged to him."[7]

## The Antitrust Movement

Not everyone felt that way. In the late 1800s, big businesses were starting to control ever-increasing amounts of the nation's resources. The larger they became, the more pressure they were able to put on their competitors. As the monopolies were able to buy out or destroy their competition, they controlled even more wealth. As these monopolies grew, working conditions deteriorated. Such conduct led many people to refer to big-business leaders as "robber barons."

Several writers of the time wrote articles and books to expose the conditions that the employees of these plants and factories were forced to endure. Among the best-known of these works are *History of the Standard Oil Company*, by Ida M. Tarbell; *The Jungle*, by Upton Sinclair; *Frenzied Finance*, by Thomas Lawson; and *The Railroads on Trial*, by Ray Stannard Baker.

Many government officials believed that it was wrong for one company to monopolize, or control, an entire industry. So they went to work to make laws that would limit the power of big business. On July 2, 1890, Congress passed the Sherman Antitrust Act. It made any business merger, combination, or trust illegal if its actions could be proven to restrain, or control, trade.

Standard Oil was one of the first monopolies to come under government scrutiny. The case against it went to the Ohio Supreme Court. On March 1, 1892, Standard Oil was found guilty of attempting to "establish a virtual monopoly."[8] Still, the ruling did not stop Rockefeller from controlling America's oil supply. To get around the court order to break up his company, he merely reorganized it and moved Standard Oil's headquarters to New Jersey.

## Theodore Roosevelt Fights Monopolies

President Theodore Roosevelt, who held office from 1901 to 1909, earned the title of Trust Buster for his efforts to put an end to harmful monopolies. Roosevelt lashed out against the "tyranny of mere wealth," and bemoaned the fact that

> the total absence of government control had led to the portentous growth . . . of . . . corporations. . . . The power of the mighty industrial overlords of the country has increased with great strides, while the method of controlling them, or checking abuses . . . remained . . . practically impotent.[9]

THE CAPTAINS OF INDUSTRY . . . HAVE ON THE WHOLE DONE GREAT GOOD TO OUR PEOPLE. WITHOUT THEM THE MATERIAL DEVELOPMENT OF WHICH WE ARE SO JUSTLY PROUD COULD NEVER HAVE TAKEN PLACE. . . . YET IT IS ALSO TRUE THAT THERE ARE REAL AND GREAT EVILS. . . . THERE IS A WIDESPREAD CONVICTION IN THE MINDS OF THE AMERICAN PEOPLE THAT THE GREAT CORPORATIONS KNOWN AS TRUSTS ARE IN CERTAIN OF THEIR FEATURES AND TENDENCIES HURTFUL TO THE GENERAL WELFARE. THIS . . . IS BASED UPON SINCERE CONVICTION THAT COMBINATION AND CONCENTRATION SHOULD BE, NOT PROHIBITED, BUT SUPERVISED AND WITHIN REASONABLE LIMITS CONTROLLED; AND IN MY JUDGMENT THIS CONVICTION IS RIGHT.[10]

*President Theodore Roosevelt took action to prevent the formation of trusts in business. In this excerpt from his first annual message to Congress, given in December 1901, Roosevelt explained his attitude toward big business.*

Roosevelt, however, did not want to do away with big business entirely. In another speech concerning the trusts, he said, "Our aim is not to destroy the corporations; on the contrary these big aggregations are a necessary part of modern industrialism. . . . We are not attacking corporations, but endeavoring to do away with the evil in them."[11]

Roosevelt ordered his attorney general to take action against monopolies. He fought against unfair trade practices—such as railroads giving lower rates to shippers with whom they had made special deals. Roosevelt's stand against monopolies helped set in motion a new national awareness of the actions of big businesses. In 1911, two years after Roosevelt left office, the United States Supreme Court was finally able to break up the Standard Oil monopoly.

In the late 1800s, there were big changes in the way Americans lived. People who had come from generations of farmers were flocking to the cities in larger numbers than ever before. Some had been displaced by machines that could do the work

# LIFE IN THE LATE 1800S

of several men. Others were lured to the city by stories of the wonderful, exciting life that awaited them there.

Immigrants were also a big part of the expanding city population. Nearly 5 million immigrants, many of them from Europe, came to the United States in the 1800s. Even though they knew life in America's cities was not perfect, these immigrants felt it would be much better than the life of poverty they would experience if they remained in their homeland.

## Overcrowded Tenement Houses

Most newcomers to America's cities had to live in tenement houses. Diseases such as measles and smallpox soon ran rampant through the overcrowded buildings. At the time, the causes of these diseases and the ways in which they were spread were not understood. Most immigrant workers could not afford the service of doctors, and they had to take care of one another the best they could.

As a result, the death rate of both immigrant adults and immigrant children was much higher than that for native-born Americans. Nearly one quarter of the children born in American cities in the late 1900s died during their first year of life.[1]

For a while, few people outside of the city were aware of these wretched conditions. That gradually began to change. By the late 1800s, several prominent writers had taken up the cause of making the general public aware of the situation. Among them were Jacob Riis, who wrote *How the Other Half Lives*, and Lincoln Steffens, author of *The Shame of the Cities*.

Another result of this overcrowding, combined with unsafe disposal of factory waste, was air and water pollution. These had already become serious problems in 1880 when a Chicago *Times* reporter wrote, "The river stinks. The air stinks. People's clothing, penetrated by the foul atmosphere, stinks. No other word expresses it so well as stink."[2]

Even prestigious magazines like *Harper's Weekly* helped expose the conditions that tenement dwellers were forced to endure. In 1876, an article in *Harper's Weekly* stated,

> half a million men, women and children are living in the tenement houses of New York. . . . No brush could paint or pencil describe . . . the utter wretchedness and misery, the vice and crime, that may be found within a stone's throw of City Hall, even within an arm's length of many churches. . . . From the nearly 200,000 tenement houses come 93 percent of the deaths and 90 percent of the crimes of our population.[3]

*The tenement houses of the crowded cities became violent, unsanitary places to live. City officials were forced to take action in an attempt to improve the situation. Here, New York City Tenement Housing Department officials inspect a cluttered basement, which a family is using for a living room.*

With all the publicity about living conditions in city tenements, politicians were forced to take action. But even though laws were passed to improve the situation, they were rarely enforced.

American-born factory workers who could afford to pay a little more for rent lived in boardinghouses. Few factory workers of the time could afford a home of their own, and a room at a boardinghouse was the next best thing. While boardinghouses furnished relatively small living quarters, they were generally cleaner and safer than the cities' tenements.

## The Brighter Side of City Life

Aside from the many problems, cities had a lot to offer. In addition to job opportunities, the bright, exciting side of city life drew newcomers by the thousands. There were newly constructed skyscrapers that rose twenty stories into the sky, towering above all the poverty and filth. There were shiny steel bridges that made it possible for people to pass across a river without the use of a boat. There were the dazzling new electric lights that lit up the nighttime sky.

The streets of America's cities in the late 1800s were filled with people. Some walked to their destinations. Others used every kind of vehicle imaginable. There were still plenty of horses and buggies on city streets in the late 1800s, but things were starting to change. New forms of transportation were starting to make their appearance.

The late 1800s saw the emergence of bicycles. During the 1890s, nearly 10 million people took up bicycle riding. Everyone from businessmen to ladies in long skirts could be seen riding bicycles around town. By 1895, an estimated 189,000 people were riding bicycles in New York City alone.[4]

*Bicycles became a popular new form of transportation in the late 1800s.*

This gave rise to the new industry of bicycle manufacturing. By 1896, three hundred American bicycle factories were turning out nearly a million bicycles a year.[5]

## Women in the Industrial Revolution

In the final decades of the 1800s, many new jobs opened up for women. Many of these jobs were in the mills or the garment industry. Ready-made clothes were in great demand. Women, working at home or in factories, were usually employed to cut the material and assemble the garments.

The introduction of the sewing machine in the mid-1800s had revolutionized the way garments were made. It cut the time women had to spend sewing for their family. Sewing machines had also made it possible for women who earned their living by sewing to take on more work and make more money.

Still, the income from sewing and from other women's occupations was far less than that earned by men. An article published in 1868 stated that a woman in Lee, Massachusetts, had earned nine hundred dollars in five years by using a sewing machine. Elizabeth Cady Stanton and Susan B. Anthony, the editors of the feminist paper, *The Revolution*, replied, "We wonder if a man can be found, who would be content with earning $900 for five years' work."[6]

*With the onset of the Industrial Revolution, more and more jobs became available outside the home for women. Here, women are assembling dolls in a factory in Philadelphia.*

By 1870, about forty thousand New York women worked full-time. Most had jobs sewing garments, either at home or in a factory. Women could also take jobs as shop girls, secretaries, telephone operators, teachers, nannies, cooks, maids, and general domestic helpers.

## Street Peddlers

Some people who lived in the city found an alternative to working in factories or offices. They made their living as street peddlers. In the mid-1800s, New York and other large cities were filled with peddlers who sold fish, newspapers, matches, fruits and vegetables, milk, and wood, and provided such services as knife sharpening. They cried out to nearby pedestrians to buy their goods. Shouts of "Fresh fish!" "Peanuts!" "Hot corn!" "Wood!" and "Buy a *Tribune!*" echoed up and down the streets and avenues of the nation's crowded cities.

*The cities bustled with activity as people bought goods from street peddlers or from outdoor markets along the street, as the people in this photograph are doing in Washington, D.C.*

Many of these street peddlers were children. In his book *Lights and Shadows of New York*, James McCabe wrote, "Little girls are numerous among the street vendors. They sell matches, tooth-picks, cigars, newspapers, songs and flowers."[7]

## Children and Public Education

While many children still had to work to help support their families in the late 1800s, more children than ever had the opportunity to attend public schools. In 1898, nearly 15 million American children were attending public schools. By that time, thirty-one states had passed laws requiring all children to attend school through the elementary grades.[8]

The new interest in education in the late 1800s also increased the demand for high schools. One educator of the time declared that "The high school is the institution which shall level the distinction between the rich and the poor . . . [thus allowing the laborer's boy] to stand alongside the rich man's son."[9] In 1870, only five hundred high schools existed in America. By the turn of the century, six thousand had been built.

Colleges were also on the increase. They were built with the aid of both public and private funds. At the end of the century, nearly a thousand colleges had been set up across the nation. While the expense of attending college was still beyond the reach of many families, approximately 238,000 students were able to enroll in college by 1900.[10]

## Looking Toward the Future

Whatever their station in life, Americans who lived in the late 1800s had witnessed the rapid changes and the marvelous inventions that the Industrial Revolution had brought to their lives. They looked to the twentieth century with hopes of an even better and brighter future.

In the early 1900s, America's cities were growing larger and were bustling with activity. They were filled with every kind of people and business. O. O. McIntire, a newspaper columnist, described New York City's Fifth Avenue in this way:

# INTO THE TWENTIETH CENTURY

> It is the "avenue of avenues.". . . No two blocks are the same for Fifth Avenue ripples along blithely from the sublime to the ridiculous. Across from the great stone lions to guard the public library gleams the red front of a five-and-ten [cent store]. . . . And in the shadow of the resplendent [rich people's] drawing rooms, the tenement poor picnic on the grassy plots of Central Park.[1]

## The Middle Class

Between the fortunes of the rich and the destitution of the poor, a new American middle class was beginning to emerge. The middle-income class was made up of people who had high-paying jobs that enabled them to raise their standard of living above that of their parents and grandparents.

Many of the people who made up the middle class worked at skilled jobs such as managing a factory, or owned small businesses. They generally bought homes in the better parts of town, far away from the dirty tenements of the inner city. Areas outside the city limits, which became known as the suburbs, were also popular with middle-class home buyers.

The new middle class had more disposable income than their parents. In addition, consumer credit, which allowed people to purchase items on a payment plan, was just coming into existence. This created a market for a new kind of product for factories to manufacture. It was a market for consumer goods—items that were purchased because of a want instead of a need. Advertisements of the time reflected the fact that people in the middle class wanted to buy items that they could live without but that made life easier and more enjoyable.

Household appliances that helped lighten the workload of women became popular at this time. Washing machines, sewing machines, and other labor-saving devices were soon commonplace in middle-class homes. An advertisement for a washing machine featured in the February 7, 1920, issue of *Literary Digest* read:

With an Automatic Electric Washer in your home you are forever free from worry over the unreliability, the whims and the changes of laundresses. . . . the heaviest blankets can be washed in a few minutes, yet the action is so gentle that it cannot harm the finest lingerie. . . . Every lamp socket is a power station, ready at the snap of a switch to run your Automatic. Costs only a trifle to operate.[2]

## Women, Minorities, and Children

In the early twentieth century, 95 percent of working women quit their jobs once they were married. The common belief was that after a woman married, she should devote her energy to taking care of the house and raising her children.

Single women often worked as typists, secretaries, telephone operators, textile and garment workers, bookkeepers, or household help. These young ladies made up over one fourth of the urban workforce, but were paid only about half of what men earned. This limited income forced them to live at home with their parents or rent a small room in a boardinghouse near the company that employed them.

Nearly 1.7 million children still had to work to help support their families at the turn of century. "Absolute necessity," a union leader of the time said, "compels the father . . . to take the child into the mine to assist him in winning bread for the family."[3]

Young boys employed by mines were often required to work sixty hours a week, but earned only a third as much money as their fathers.

Women and children were not the only ones who were underpaid. In the early 1900s, it was common practice for business to routinely discriminate against African Americans and other minorities. Most had no choice but to work for low wages as janitors, dishwashers, food servers, and in other service jobs. As a result, four times as many married black women as white women had to work outside of the home to help make ends meet.

However, a few African-American professionals were able to find well-paying jobs in the cities. Some African Americans were even able to come up with the money to start their own business, primarily in African-American neighborhoods. They opened grocery and clothing stores, barber shops, laundries, and other community businesses, primarily serving African-American customers, who could not always get good service from white business owners. Many of these African-American businesses were successful and earned a nice profit for their owners. They also provided employment for African Americans who would probably have a difficult time finding similar work in the white community.

## The Age of the Automobile

As the 1800s came to a close, steam engines, electrical motors, and gas engines were used for all kinds of industrial applications. But aside from ships and trains, public transportation had not benefited from any of those sources of power. While a small number of wealthy people had been able to obtain specially built gas, steam, or electrical motor-driven cars, the vast majority of Americans got around town by walking,

*Modern vehicles made life easier for city residents, but they also caused new types of hazards. This drawing from Leslie's Weekly in 1895 shows an ambulance arriving after a man was hit by a street car.*

pedaling a bicycle, riding on a horse, or riding in a horse-drawn carriage.

At the time, there were only about five thousand automobiles on American roads. Some had been brought over from Europe. Others had been built in America by companies such as Olds. All were very expensive, and only the well-to-do had enough money to buy one.

However, all of that was about to change. Several inventors were hard at work designing power-driven street vehicles that could be mass-produced in factories and sold at a reasonable price.

Henry Ford, a mechanic and the chief engineer of the Edison Light Company in Detroit, believed that motor-powered vehicles could be built at a price the ordinary person could afford.

Ford saw a ready market for a rugged, practical car—one that the average American farmer, factory worker, or shopkeeper could afford. He set out to prove that such a car could be built in America.

Ford set up a workshop in a shed beside his home. There, in his free time, he designed and built his first automobile. By 1893, Ford's two-cylinder car was finished and ready to drive.

Ford continued to improve upon his idea for an inexpensive motor vehicle. Then in 1901, he decided that it was time to draw attention to his new product.

*Henry Ford worked to bring an affordable and practical automobile to people all over America.*

He challenged Alexander Winton, a wealthy man who owned a sleek race car, to a race at Grosse Point, Michigan. Ford's car won. The top speed was clocked at nearly forty-four miles per hour.

In 1903, Henry Ford formed the Ford Motor Company. Using twenty-eight thousand dollars in investment capital, he had his first automobile factory built in Michigan.

Five years later, in 1908, the Ford Motor Company introduced the Model T, also known as the Tin Lizzie. The Model T ran on four cylinders and could travel about twenty miles on a gallon of gasoline.

These cars were not generally considered beautiful. They were all painted black, and every Model T that came off Ford's assembly line looked exactly like all the others. But Model T cars were sturdy enough to drive on rough country roads, and they were relatively easy to repair if they broke down.

In the beginning, Ford's car caused a commotion whenever he took it out for a drive. Most people had never seen an automobile before. Ford recalled:

> It was considered something of a nuisance, for it made a racket and scared horses. Also it blocked traffic. For if I stopped my machine anywhere in town a crowd was around it before I could start up again. If I left it alone, even for a minute, some inquisitive person was always trying to run it. Finally I had to carry a chain, and chain it to a lamp post whenever I left it anywhere.[4]

When it was first introduced, the Model T was priced at $950. While this was still too much for the average person to pay for a car, it was far less than any other company was charging. Ford still continued to look for ways to improve his production technique and make cars less expensive.

In 1913, Ford introduced an innovative assembly system that delivered the car to the workers. As the car frame came down the assembly line, workers added a piece at each stop. Every worker knew his task by heart and performed it automatically as the car stopped at his station. By the time the car arrived at the end of the assembly line, it was complete and ready to drive. This cut the time needed to build a car, from fourteen hours to an hour and a half. It made affordable automobiles a reality.

Ford's factory was a success. Everyone who could afford a Tin Lizzie wanted one. As time went by, Ford's cars became even more affordable. A new Model T that cost $600 in 1912 could be purchased for only $290 in 1924.[5] By 1927, the Ford Motor Company had sold over 15 million Model T cars.[6] Soon, other automobile manufacturers such as General Motors decided to use Ford's production techniques in their own factories.

| Motor Vehicle Registration and Sales, 1900–1930 | | |
|---|---|---|
| Year | Motor Vehicle Registration | Factory Sales |
| 1900 | 8,000 | 4,100 |
| 1905 | 78,000 | 24,200 |
| 1910 | 468,500 | 181,000 |
| 1915 | 2,490,000 | 895,900 |
| 1920 | 9,239,100 | 1,905,500 |
| 1925 | 20,068,500 | 3,735,100 |
| (Source: Historical Statistics of the United States) | | |

*As Ford and his factory were able to make cars more affordable for the average person, automobiles quickly became more popular, and with them, traffic became more congested. Here, a policeman directs traffic in downtown Chicago.*

## The Second Industrial Revolution

The second Industrial Revolution, from 1910 to 1950, saw a marked growth in the manufacture of consumer goods. Whereas the first Industrial Revolution was powered primarily by steam engines, electricity was now the major source of power.

After the turn of the century, electric power was available in many American cities and towns. Lighting streets and running industrial machinery was only the beginning of what electricity could do. The rapid expansion of electric power stations throughout the nation opened a market for an entirely different type of invention—products that were powered by electricity.

Middle-class families living in the early 1900s filled their homes with modern inventions such as electric lamps and phonographs. These were things that no one, no matter how wealthy, would have dreamed of owning only a few decades earlier.

When radios came into common use in the 1920s, even people who lived in the most isolated regions of America could keep up with what was happening around the world. By putting on a headset and turning a few knobs, one could hear programs broadcast from cities many miles away. News that would otherwise take days, if not weeks, to arrive could be heard instantaneously.

This interest in tuning in to radio programs created a brand-new industry. In the beginning, most radios were built by amateur radio operators in their spare time. But now that the demand was big, factories all over the nation worked overtime to produce radios. For the first few years, they could not keep up with the demand. Everyone who could afford it wanted a radio of their own.

Before long, radios were the centerpiece of living rooms all over the nation. Families gathered around the radio in the evening to hear music, news, and entertainment programs that were now available to anyone who had a radio receiver.

Then, industry found another use for radio. To help promote their products, they agreed to sponsor, or help pay for, popular programs. Everything from soap and medicine to washing machines and breakfast cereal was advertised on radio. In most cases, these ad campaigns were successful. They caught the public attention and helped boost product sales.

## World War I Speeds Industrialization

In the first half of the twentieth century, the United States was involved in two world wars. These wars brought with them the demand for faster ways to mass-produce goods. The military needed everything from vehicles and weapons to uniforms—and they needed them as quickly as possible.

At the start of World War I, the United States government did not know how much steel, or how many weapons and other necessary goods, American industries were capable of producing, so they formed a War Industry Board to help deal with the problem. In March 1918, President Woodrow Wilson appointed stock speculator Bernard M. Baruch to head the board. Throughout the war, he worked with industrial leaders to make certain that the military had the supplies it needed to win the war. Hundreds of industries, including Ford, General Motors, General Electric, U.S. Steel, and Standard Oil, took part in the program and were given contracts from the government to manufacture the products it needed.[7]

During World War I, many of the men who had once worked in factories went into the armed service. It was during this time, when extra factory labor was needed, that many married women first entered the industrial workforce.

To make sure that the military could move troops, supplies, and other equipment across the country as quickly as possible, the United States government decided to take over control of the nation's railroad systems. In December 1917, the secretary of the treasury, William G. MacAdoo, was put in charge of managing them. Until the war was over, the military's needs took priority over general industrial orders, civilian passengers, and anything else that needed to be transported by train. Services MacAdoo deemed unnecessary were halted completely.

The United States military was also in dire need of ships for the war effort. Charles M. Schwab, a leader in the nation's steel industry, organized the Shipping Board and the Emergency Fleet Corporation. By the time World War I was over, more than a hundred warships and numerous merchant ships had been built under his direction.[8]

World War I also saw the first large-scale industrial production of airplanes. Fleets of small biplanes, known as jennies, were put into service to teach American pilots how to fight air wars against the planes of Germany.

## Life Between the Wars

After the United States and its allies won World War I, many Americans felt optimistic enough about their economic future to buy on payment plans items they could not otherwise afford. During the 1920s, consumer debt rose 250 percent. Many of those who were fortunate enough to have more money than they needed to support themselves invested in the stock market. This rapid increase in product sales and heavy investment in the stock market caused the value of stocks to climb much higher than their actual worth.

In addition, nations all over the world were struggling financially. The Treaty of Versailles, which ended World War I, made Germany and the other defeated nations pay huge sums of money as punishment for starting the war. This caused terrible inflation all over Europe, as well as financial instability, which began to affect the whole world.

This could only go on for so long. In 1929, the American stock market crashed, throwing the United States into the worst economic depression it had ever experienced. Over 12 million people lost their jobs when businesses closed or cut back on production. As people struggled to keep their homes and feed their families, the consumer goods made available in recent years became less important, and businesses continued to fail.

## The New Deal

When President Franklin D. Roosevelt came into office at the height of the Great Depression in 1932, he instituted a policy that he hoped would bring the

*After the onset of the Great Depression, people struggled just to feed and shelter their families. Many depended on soup kitchens like this one for food.*

nation back to prosperity. He called this program the New Deal.

While the New Deal was designed to help businesses get back on their feet, it also benefited labor unions and industrial workers. The National Recovery Act, passed in 1933, attempted to shorten the workday, raise wages, outlaw child labor, and guarantee the rights of labor unions. Though the act was overturned by the Supreme Court, it formed the basis for later laws that would be passed to protect workers. These laws included the Wagner Act of 1935 and the Fair Labor Standards Act of 1938.

Among other things, these laws guaranteed the right of labor unions to bargain with employers, and forbade companies to fire or discriminate against employees for belonging to unions. Now that their organizations were supported by federal laws, union leaders went to work recruiting new members. The American Federation of Labor (AFL) and the Congress of Industrial Organizations (CIO) were especially active during this time. By 1940, 9 million people had joined labor unions.[9]

In addition to promoting the growth of unions, Roosevelt helped American workers by instituting government job programs such as the Civil Works Administration and the Civilian Conservation Corps. These programs created jobs for many people who could not otherwise find work during the Great Depression.

## America Enters World War II

World War II brought new challenges to America's industries. As with World War I, the military needed factories to produce weapons, tanks, uniforms, and other wartime necessities faster than before. In 1938 and 1939, President Roosevelt signed two important bills to strengthen America's military. The first of these bills, the Vinson Naval Act, appropriated a billion dollars for the construction of new warships. A year later, Congress approved another $2 billion for American industries to build more ships, arms, weapons, and airplanes.[10] After that, America's military was unquestionably the best equipped in the world.

## Opportunities for Women and Minorities

With so many men serving in the military, factory owners often had a difficult time finding enough workers to operate their machinery. To keep up with their production schedules, they decided to hire women.

With the prompting of popular songs of the time such as "Rosie the Riveter" and "We're the Janes That Make the Planes," women who had never considered employment outside of the home before discovered that they could weld metal, tend a blast furnace, operate a crane, load ammunition, and perform a wide variety of other jobs that had previously been available only to men. Most defense-industry jobs paid higher wages than traditional women's occupations such as teaching and typing.

Many women enjoyed the challenge of their new occupations. Inez Sauer, who went to work for Boeing, a company that manufactures aircraft in Seattle, Washington, said,

> At Boeing, I found a freedom and an independence I had never known. After the war, I could never go back to playing bridge again, being a clubwoman and listening to a lot of inanities [silly things] when I knew there were things you would use your mind for. The war changed my life completely.[11]

In all, over 6 million women took jobs during World War II, which increased the total number of working women in the United States to 19 million. Approximately 75 percent of them were married, and over 33 percent had children under the age of fourteen.[12]

Minorities also benefited from the need for extra factory workers. Nearly 2 million African Americans were able to get industrial jobs during World War II. Many Mexican Americans and American Indians were also hired to work in jobs that had not been open to them previously.[13]

This increase in jobs for minorities was partly due to an executive order issued by President Roosevelt in June 1941. This order prohibited any factory, union, or federal agency involved in the war effort from discriminating against job applicants on account of their race. When word got out about the new job opportunities, over a million African Americans left the South and came to industrial cities in the North to start a new life. Four years after the law went into effect, the number of African Americans working for war-related industries had increased from 3 percent to 9 percent.[14]

African Americans and other minorities had made some big progress in becoming an accepted part of the American workforce. For women, however, the changes were only temporary. As soon as the war was over, the majority of women gave up their jobs and returned to their roles as housewives. Even those who wanted to continue working were often forced to quit when male veterans returned from the war to reclaim their old jobs at the factories.

# THE INDUSTRIAL LEGACY

More than anything else in the past, the Industrial Revolution changed the world in dramatic ways. In under two hundred years, it completely transformed the way people lived, how they worked, and the way the products they used were made.

The mass-production techniques of the Industrial Revolution made it possible for factories to produce goods many times faster than the goods could be made by hand. Rapid production also allowed businesses to sell their goods for lower prices. This elevated the standard of living by making items such as ready-made clothing, wool rugs, fancy cookware, and preprocessed food available to people who could not have been able to afford them otherwise.

The discoveries and great technological progress made during this time led to the creation of new methods of transportation and communication that

*The innovations of the Industrial Revolution made life easier, and many, like the automobile, made farmers feel less isolated from nearby towns and cities.*

no one could have dreamed possible in the past. Telephones allowed the human voice to be heard miles away. Steamboats revolutionized river transportation. And railroads made it possible for farmers and factory owners to transport their goods to customers thousands of miles away at a reasonable price.

The Industrial Revolution made life easier and more exciting in many ways. But the telephones, televisions, radios, automobiles, airplanes, and other inventions that came into use during the later years of the Industrial Revolution did something else, too. They took away the isolation of the single-family farm, and made communication with neighbors, friends, and even strangers around the world possible. They opened the horizons of nearly every American to the sights, sounds, and thoughts of people they might never have known without them.

# ★ Timeline ★

**1712**—Thomas Newcomen invents the first practical steam engine.

**1733**—John Kay invents the flying shuttle to speed the weaving process.

**1764**—James Watt improves on Newcomen's steam-engine design.

**1769**—Richard Arkwright invents the spinning frame.

**1781**—James Watt makes further improvements on the steam engine.

**1787**—John Fitch operates a passenger steamboat service in New England.

**1789**—Samuel Slater moves to America with the knowledge of how to mass-produce thread.

**1790**—The first American patent law is enacted.

**1791**—Alexander Hamilton presents his *Report on Manufactures* to Congress.

**1793**—Eli Whitney invents the cotton gin.

**1807**—Robert Fulton launches the first commercially successful steamboat.

**1818**—The Erie Canal is built in New York State.
**–1825**

**1844**—Samuel Morse sends the first telegraph message between cities.

**1846**—The first sewing machine is patented by Elias Howe.

**1846**
**–1854**—Thousands of European immigrants come to America to find factory work.

**1856**—Englishman Henry Bessemer discovers a better method of manufacturing steel.

**1859**—The first American oil well is drilled in Pennsylvania.

**1866**—The National Labor Union (NLU) is formed.

**1867**—Christopher Latham introduces the first commercially successful typewriter.

**1869**—America's first transcontinental railroad is completed.

**1870**—John D. Rockefeller incorporates Standard Oil of Ohio.

**1873**—Andrew Carnegie opens the world's largest steel mill in Pennsylvania.

**1876**—The Centennial Exhibition in Philadelphia, Pennsylvania, displays America's first hundred years of industrial progress; Alexander Graham Bell patents the telephone.

**1877**—A cut in railroad-workers' pay sets off violent strikes; Thomas Alva Edison invents the phonograph.

**1879**—Thomas Edison invents the incandescent light bulb.

**1882**—The Standard Oil Company becomes the first trust in America.

**1908**—The Ford Motor Company introduces the Model T, America's first popular automobile.

**1917**—World War I spurs American industry on to
**–1918** greater production.

**1929**—The stock market crashes, sending the nation into the Great Depression.

**1932**—Franklin D. Roosevelt wins the presidential election and institutes his New Deal programs to help the economy get back on track.

**1941**—World War II revitalizes American industry;
**–1945** Women and minorities enter the workforce in large numbers.

**1946**—After World War II ends, many of the production techniques developed for the war effort are used to manufacture consumer products.

# ★ CHAPTER NOTES ★

## Chapter 1. A Century of Progress

1. Dee Brown, *The Year of the Century: 1876* (New York: Charles Scribner's Sons, 1966), p. 114.

2. Copylab Publishing Council, Inc., *The United States Encyclopedia of History* (New York: Curtis Publishing Company, 1967), vol. 4, p. 720.

3. Brown, p. 129.

4. Robert Silverberg, *Light for the World: Edison and the Power Industry* (Princeton, N.J.: D. Van Nostrand Company, Inc., 1967), p. 10.

## Chapter 2. The Revolution Begins

1. Walter Buehr, *Cloth: From Fiber to Fabric* (New York: William Morrow and Company, 1965), p. 38.

2. Penny Clarke, *Growing Up During the Industrial Revolution* (London: B. T. Batsford, Ltd., 1982), p. 40.

3. Isaac Asimov, *Asimov's Chronology of Science & Discovery* (New York: HarperCollins Publishers, Inc., 1994), p. 255.

## Chapter 3. Industry in America

1. Edward Hugh Cameron, *Samuel Slater: Father of American Manufacturers* (Portland, Maine: Bond Wheelright Company, 1960), p. 37.

2. Jeanette Mirsky and Allan Nevins, *The World of Eli Whitney* (New York: Macmillan Company, 1952), p. 62.

3. George Brown Tindall, *America: A Narrative History* (New York: W. W. Norton & Company, Inc., 1984), p. 290.

4. Ibid., p. 295, quoting Thomas Jefferson, *Notes on Virginia,* 1785.

5. James West Davidson et al., *Nation of Nations* (New York: McGraw-Hill, 1989), vol. 1, p. 342.

6. Mirsky and Nevins, p. 138.

## Chapter 4. The Factory System

1. Benita Eisler, ed., *The Lowell Offering: Writings by New England Mill Women (1840–1845)* (Philadelphia; New York: J. B. Lippincott Company, 1977), p. 19.

2. Ibid., p. 18.

3. James West Davidson et al., *Nation of Nations: A Concise Narrative of the American Republic* (New York: Overture Books, 1996), p. 259.

4. George Soule, *Economic Forces in American History* (Bennington, Vt.: Dryden Press, 1952), p. 128.

5. George Brown Tindall, *America: A Narrative History* (New York: W. W. Norton & Company, Inc., 1984), p. 452.

6. George Rogers Taylor, *The Economic History of the United States, The Transportation Revolution 1815–1860* (New York: Rinehart & Company, Inc., 1951), vol. 6, pp. 284–285.

7. Davidson et al., p. 483.

8. Ibid., p. 484.

9. Marc McCutcheon, *The Writer's Guide to Everyday Life in the 1800s* (Cincinnati: Writer's Digest Books, 1993), p. 131.

10. Ibid., p. 62.

11. Ibid., p. 129.

## Chapter 5. Roads, Boats, and Railroads

1. George Rogers Taylor, *The Economic History of the United States, vol. IV, The Transportation Revolution 1815–1860* (New York: Rinehart & Company, Inc., 1951), vol. 6, pp. 132–133.

2. Ibid., p. 19.

3. Ibid.

4. Ibid., p. 25.

5. Ibid., p. 27.

6. Franklin M. Reck, *The Romance of American Transportation*, rev. ed. (New York: Thomas Y. Crowell Company, 1962), p. 20.

7. Ibid., pp. 12, 13.

8. In David Colbert, ed., *Eyewitness to America: 500 Years of America in the Words of Those Who Saw It Happen* (New York: Pantheon Books, 1997), p. 113.

9. James West Davidson et al., *Nation of Nations: A Concise Narrative of the American Republic* (New York Overture Books, 1996), p. 248.

10. Walter Havighurst, *Voices on the River* (New York: Macmillan Company, 1967), p. 53.

11. Ibid., p. 198.

12. Paul Johnson, *Birth of the Modern: World Society, 1815–1830* (New York: HarperCollins Publishers, 1991), p. 200.

13. Taylor, p. 132.

14. Reck, p. 60.

15. Edward Countryman, *The Americans: A Collection of Histories* (New York: Hill and Wang, 1996), p. 116.

16. Davidson et al., p. 248.

17. Ibid., p. 470.

## Chapter 6. New Ways to Communicate

1. E. A. Marland, *Early Electrical Communication* (London; New York; Toronto: Abelard-Schuman Ltd., 1964), p. 9, citing S. I. Prime, *Life of Samuel F. B. Morse* (New York: 1875), pp. 251–252.

2. Leroy Pagano et al., *The Rise and Progress of American Industry* (Chicago: United States Historical Society, Inc., 1970), p. 19.

3. Page Smith, *The Rise of Industrial America: A People's History of the Post-Reconstruction Era* (New York: McGraw-Hill, 1984), p. 114.

4. Marland, p. 187, quoting T. A. Watson, *Exploring Life* (New York: 1926), p. 62.

5. Claude S. Fisher, *America Calling: A Social History of the Telephone* (Berkeley; Los Angeles: University of California Press, 1992), p. 33.

6. John Brooks, *Telephone: The First Hundred Years* (New York: Harper and Row, Publishers, 1976), p. 66.

7. Ibid., p. 66.

8. Cheris Kramarae, ed., *Technology and Women's Voices: Keeping in Touch* (New York; London: Routledge & Kegan Paul, 1988), p. 213, citing an illustration of an advertisement from the D'Arcy Collection.

9. Ibid., p. 217.

10. Richie Calder, *The Evolution of the Machine* (New York: American Heritage Publishing Co., Inc., 1968), p. 96.

11. Robert Silverberg, *Light for the World: Edison and the Power Industry* (Princeton, N.J.: D. Van Nostrand Company, Inc., 1967), p. 106.

12. In David Colbert, ed., *Eyewitness to America: 500 Years of America in the Words of Those Who Saw It Happen* (New York: Pantheon Books, 1997), p. 281.

13. Ibid., p. 182.

14. Robert Friedel and Paul Israel, *Edison's Electric Light* (New Brunswick, N.J.: Rutgers University Press, 1987), p. 22.

15. Mark Truby, "Electrical Infrastructure: A City Positive, A special report—Infrastructure: The Health of Huntington," *The Herald Dispatch*, October 30, 1996, n.p.

## Chapter 7. The Age of Big Business

1. James West Davidson et al., *Nation of Nations: A Concise Narrative of the American Republic* (New York: Overture Books, 1996), p. 472.

2. Ibid., p. 473.

3. Allan Nevins and Henry Steele Commager, *A Pocket History of the United States*, 9th rev. ed.(New York: Pocket Books, 1992), p. 266.

4. Robert L. Heilbroner, "Carnegie & Rockefeller," *A Sense of History: The Best Writings from the Pages of American Heritage* (New York: American Heritage Press, Inc., 1985), p. 441.

5. Ibid.

6. Ibid., p. 439.

7. Stanley Buder, *Pullman: An Experiment in Industrial Order and Community Planning, 1880–1930* (New York: Oxford University Press, 1967), p. 15.

8. Leroy Pagano et al., *The Rise and Progress of American Industry* (Chicago: United States Historical Society, Inc., 1970), p. 35.

9. Nathan Miller, *Theodore Roosevelt: A Life* (New York: William Morrow and Company, Inc., 1992), p. 366.

10. In William A. DeGregorio, *The Complete Book of U.S. Presidents* (New York: Dembner Books, 1984) pp. 385–386.

11. Nevins and Commager, p. 276.

## Chapter 8. Life in the Late 1800s

1. James West Davidson et al., *Nation of Nations: A Concise Narrative of the American Republic* (New York: Overture Books, 1996), p. 497.

2. *This Fabulous Century: Prelude 1870–1900* (New York: Time-Life Books, 1970), p. 220.

3. Marc McCutcheon, *The Writer's Guide to Everyday Life in the 1800s* (Cincinnati: Writer's Digest Books, 1993), p. 101.

4. O. O. McIntyre, *The "Odd" Book: Selected Short Stories and Columns*, comp. and annot. Laura E. Kratz, Ph.D. (Gallipolis, Ohio: Gallia County Historical Society, 1989), p. 23.

5. *This Fabulous Century: Prelude 1870–1900*, p. 120.

6. Cheris Kramarae, ed., *Technology and Women's Voices: Keeping in Touch* (New York; London: Routledge & Kegan Paul, 1988), p. 151.

7. McCutcheon, p. 137.

8. *This Fabulous Century: Prelude 1870–1900*, p. 142.

9. Ibid., p. 142.

10. Ibid.

## Chapter 9. Into the Twentieth Century

1. O. O. McIntyre, *The "Odd" Book: Selected Short Stories and Columns*, comp. and annot. Laura E. Kratz, Ph.D. (Gallipolis, Ohio: Gallia County Historical Society, 1989), p. 37.

2. Cheris Kramarae, ed., *Technology and Women's Voices: Keeping in Touch* (New York; London: Routledge & Kegan Paul, 1988), p. 168.

3. James West Davidson et al., *Nation of Nations: A Concise Narrative of the American Republic* (New York: Overture Books, 1996), p. 481.

4. Allan Nevins and Henry Steele Commager, *A Pocket History of the United States*, 9th rev. ed. (New York: Pocket Books, 1992), p. 259.

5. Gary B. Nash et al., *The American People: Creating a Nation and Society*, 3rd ed. (New York: HarperCollins College Publishers, 1994), p. 788.

6. Leroy Pagano et al., *The Rise and Progress of American Industry* (Chicago: United States Historical Society, Inc., 1970), p. 45.

7. Ibid., p. 52.

8. Ibid.

9. Nevins and Commager, p. 424.

10. Leroy Pagano et al., p. 58.

11. Paul S. Boyer et al., *The Enduring Vision* (Lexington, Mass.: D.C. Heath and Company, 1993), p. 914.

12. Ibid., p. 913.

13. Ibid., p. 915.

14. Ibid.

# ★ FURTHER READING ★

## Books

Brooks, John. *Telephone: The First Hundred Years*. New York: Harper and Row, Publishers, 1976.

Calder, Richie. *The Evolution of the Machine*. New York: American Heritage Publishing Co., Inc., 1968.

Clarke, Penny. *Growing Up During the Industrial Revolution*. London: B. T. Batsford, Ltd., 1982.

Davidson, James West, et al. *Nation of Nations: A Concise Narrative of the American Republic*. New York: Overture Books, 1996.

Eisler, Benita, ed. *The Lowell Offering: Writings by New England Mill Women (1840–1845)*. Philadelphia: J. B. Lippincott Company, 1977.

Fanning, Leonard M. Men, *Money and Oil: The Story of Industry*. Cleveland: World Publishing Company, 1966.

Fremon, David K. *The Great Depression in American History*. Springfield, N.J.: Enslow Publishers, Inc., 1997.

Harris, Jacqueline L. *Henry Ford*. New York: Franklin Watts, 1984.

Hoag, Edwin. *American Cities: Their Historical and Social Development*. Philadelphia: J. B. Lippincott Company, 1969.

Knox, Diana. *The Industrial Revolution*. St. Paul, Minn.: Greenhaven Press, Inc., 1980.

Kramarae, Cheris, ed. *Technology and Women's Voices: Keeping in Touch*. New York: Routledge & Kegan Paul, 1988.

Miner, Lewis S. *Industrial Genius: Samuel Slater*. New York: Julian Messner, 1968.

Neal, Harry Edward. *From Spinning Wheel to Space Craft: The Story of the Industrial Revolution*. New York: Julian Messner, 1964.

Pagano, Leroy, et al. *The Rise and Progress of American Industry*. Chicago: United States Historical Society, Inc., 1970.

Reck, Franklin M. *The Romance of American Transportation*, rev. ed. New York: Thomas Y. Crowell Company, 1962.

Silverberg, Robert. *Light for the World: Edison and the Power Industry*. Princeton, N.J.: D. Van Nostrand Company, Inc., 1967.

Stein, R. Conrad. *The Transcontinental Railroad in American History*. Springfield, N.J.: Enslow Publishers, Inc., 1997.

*This Fabulous Century: Prelude 1870–1900*. New York: Time-Life Books, 1970.

## Internet Addresses

Halsall, Paul. "Industrial Revolution." *Internet Modern History Sourcebook*. 1997. <http://www.fordham.edu/halsall/mod/modsbook14.html>.

*Turn of the Century in U.S. History*. n.d. <http://www.ushistory.net//toc>.

# ★ INDEX ★